REIGNITE YOUR RELATIONSHIP BY 7X:

So you can get back to making love and enjoying your spouse

By Marshaun Olaniyan

Copyright © 2019 Marshaun Olaniyan

All rights reserved.

All rights reserved. No part of this publication may be reproduced, stored in a retrieval system, or transmitted in any form or by any means, without the prior permission in writing from the author.

ISBN-13: 978-1-948777-07-0
ISBN-10: 1-948777-07-X

Visit my website to set up a FREE Discovery Call for a step by step plan to create your love life ©
www.marshaunolaniyan.com

Get more awesome content on how to create a healthy romantic relationship at:
www.youtube.com/marshauno

Why I Wrote This Book

I wrote this book because I wish I had not experienced a divorce. I wish I never had to go through the dating phase again trying to figure things out on my own. I wrote this because I did not receive the proper guidance from my parents when it came to knowing or understanding myself. The real me. The person who was proud to look at herself in the mirror and know who she was. I wrote this book because I once had low self-esteem, didn't love my own skin and chose the wrong men to whom I gave my mind, body and partial soul. Coupled with the fact that I had low self-esteem and I did not receive the proper talks about love, dating, relationships, and especially marriage, I knocked my head too many times to think about. I wrote this book because even though I experienced things in life and love that I did not like or think should have been a part of my life's story, it was all a part of my destiny. I wrote this book because I can help men and women see the beauty in love and how to implement simple yet effective tips and proven strategies into their love life. Then they, too, can create an awesome love story. I wrote this book because I did the work, collected the data, and used these same tips and strategies within my own relationship. I have figured out the secrets not only to creating a love story but also to living within an awesome love story.

Why You Should Read This Book

Being in a relationship (be it romantic or otherwise) for any period of time can result in having a few misunderstandings, dealing with your own ego and prideful behavior and not saying *I'm sorry* as much as you should. It also includes being intentional, being respectful, and having those tough conversations with your partner. Each of these things, both the good and the bad, are all a part of the process of developing a relationship in which you are often in a state of blissfulness and utter joy.

Many of us want to have that type of relationship where everyone notices and is just a bit envious of the bond in our relationship. We want others to see us (you and your spouse) as the "it" couple. It's okay! We all like to be celebrated by others. I once heard a saying that "people will celebrate you openly for what you've done in private for years." This statement resonates with truth! It takes years to build a deep and tightly bonded relationship in which the two of you are relying almost solely on each other, not needing to look outside the relationship for others' approval or even their opinions. This is a great thing, as you should cleave to your spouse and become one flesh. You two should be each other's cheerleaders in everything each of you do no matter what, whether you agree with that thing or not.

To get there, you and your spouse must go through all the things discussed and plenty more that are not discussed in this book. Having a healthy romantic relationship takes being intentional and making sure your spouse and the relationship itself gets the nurture and care they both need. Your relationship will thrive and become more enriched the more time and effort you spend working on it.

Some people expect this type of relationship to just show up with little to no effort, but that is just not the case. A relationship like this will never just appear out of thin air. You two met, dated, got engaged and married . . . that was the easy part. The hard part now begins at making sure the two of you stay in love and connected to each other. It means saying *I'm sorry* so that the issue can be resolved and the two of you can get back to loving each other and to the happier times. It means making sure you create the time to spend with your spouse, even when you are dead tired. It means forsaking those outside forces, including family, who may try to come in between you and your spouse. It means making sure your job/career does not take all your **best fuel** throughout the day and your spouse and family are left only with the remnants. It means making sure you two are connected by continuing to date, holding hands, and showing affection toward one another. It means doing silly things you never imagined yourself doing. It means when you think about him or her, he/she is your happy place to revel in, even when you are mad at him or her because you know that this, too, shall pass. In short, it means choosing your significant other, every day, (and especially) when it seems like making that choice is hard.

Creating the relationship you desire can be done by taking small steps toward that dream every day. You create it every day and live it with the love of your life every single day. Creating this type of love happens on purpose. You have to take control, make this a priority, and watch just how deep, loving, intimate, happy, healthy and joyful the two of you will be.

Continue reading to create the love life you want with your spouse right by your side, with little to no misunderstandings, sustaining the foundation that was built on solid ground, showing gratitude, sharing much more laughter between the two of you, and being your spouse's friend. Creating the relationship you dreamed about is within the confines of this book. The best way to see results is to make sure you are taking action and implementing what you learn here: the importance of laughter, showing your love to your spouse, discussing your relationship expectations, and making time to work on the relationship together.

TABLE OF CONTENTS

Why I Wrote This Book 4

Why You Should Read This Book 5

CHAPTER 1: Love thyself and deal with
your fear and baggage 9

CHAPTER 2: Happiness is your choice 21

CHAPTER 3: Show more love, gratitude and
appreciation towards your spouse 31

CHAPTER 4: Be intentional and show
respect toward your spouse and relationship 43

CHAPTER 5: Listen as your spouse's
friend and do not try to change him or her 51

CHAPTER 6: Continue to have a life
outside of your spouse 69

CHAPTER 7: Spend quality time with yourself in
addition to your spouse 73

CHAPTER 8: Discuss these relationship
expectations: Finance, religion & children 89

CHAPTER 9: Do not focus on your
partner's negative characteristics 109

CHAPTER 10: Keep god first 115

About the Author 120

CHAPTER 1

Love thyself and deal with your fear and baggage

"Loving yourself starts with liking yourself, which starts with respecting yourself, which starts with thinking of yourself in positive ways." ~Jerry Corsten

Love thyself first. What does this mean? Some may think about a day of pampering themselves at the spa with manicures, pedicures and massages. Others may define loving thyself as getting out into nature and taking long, uninterrupted walks in the woods or along the beach. However, loving thyself requires a deeper understanding of one's self, meaning you have to find peace and accordance within yourself, be able to relax into yourself, and be comfortable in your own skin. Yes, you can find temporary relief in doing the things that nurture you outwardly, but achieving that deeper inner peace requires cultivating a certain way of being within yourself. It requires having a warm, fuzzy, nurturing attitude toward what you experience inside. You have to master the internal world before you master the external world.

Yes, you have to be loving toward your partner, but if you give all your love away, meaning your time and energy, to nurture everyone around you except you, you will burn out, become stressed, irritated, a bit depressed, and even want to stop after some time of doing these things. If you are not properly taking care of you, then you cannot fully take care of anyone else. Do not worry about what others will say about you saying "No" or not showing up to their event because you want to show love to yourself. They will understand that you could not make it this time around and even if they don't, it will still be okay.

By loving yourself, you will attract the love you seek on a deeper level. Your partner will gravitate toward you because you have recharged yourself and are now showing up even better than before. You will be happier, more playful, and will have a focus and determination to get things done. You will be able to show your love by listening to your partner without needing to be heard or by trying to solve their problem. You can be his or her shoulder to lean on.

Lisa had to learn this the hard way. Lisa and Luke had been married for five years. They had a great life together with their two-year-old son, Leon. Lisa was always running around after Leon, picking up his toys, changing diapers, washing those never-ending dishes, washing and folding up the clothes, cooking dinner, sweeping the floors and mopping them. This was just her home life. At work, she was a big-time executive for a bank. There she conducted meetings, solved all emergencies, and dealt with customer complaints. Lisa never took time off to recharge herself. She believed she could never take the time to love herself or some

CHAPTER 1

things would not get completed. She had not done this in so long that she would not know where to begin or how to relax if she did take the time to love herself and recharge. She did not have the time to get a pedicure, manicure and massage, read a book, take a relaxing bath, enjoy a movie, meditate, or the like. She hated exercising and had noticed some weight gain. Lisa also thought she could do everything herself without asking for help or delegating more of the tasks to someone else that could handle them, especially at work. She was a bit of a control freak, thinking no one could do it like her.

At home, Lisa never asked Luke to help her either, even to get a bit of relief. She believed her man should not lift a finger around the household, not even to take out the trash. Lisa certainly was setting herself up for failure. And sure enough, her day came, and when it did, it came with a vengeance! Everything came to a screeching halt when Lisa collapsed at home. After being rushed to the hospital, she was diagnosed with an anxiety or panic attack. Lisa had so much stress coming from all angles of her life that she could not deny this fact any longer. Her body could not take it any longer and forced her to sit down.

While at the hospital, after hearing the diagnosis, Luke, Lisa's husband, stepped in to ask her what he could do to make her feel loved and taken care of. He assured her that she always took care of everyone else and now he wanted to do the same for her even after she got the much-needed rest as prescribed by the doctor. Luke finally realized the impact of not helping Lisa around the house and with Leon. He vowed to never let this happen again as long as he could help it.

As you can see, you can love and give and give and give to everyone, but you must take care of yourself first! If you are not taking care of you, then you will start to resent and feel some anger and hate toward others even if it is never displayed to the outside world. You internally start to erode. You must take a break from all the drama, the to-do lists, children, spouse, and that next project. You are your own priority! You are worth taking the time to recharge! You deserve it!

These three quotes fit here perfectly.

> *The most powerful relationship you will ever have is the relationship with yourself.*
> **– Steve Maraboli, Life, the Truth, and Being Free**

> *Love is a great miracle cure. Loving ourselves works miracles in our lives.*
> **– Louise L. Hay**

> *Your task is not to seek love, but merely to seek and find all the barriers within yourself that you have built against it.*
> **– Rumi**, -thirteenth century Sufi poet

CHAPTER 1

What do you need to do to make sure you are prioritizing yourself? Make a brief list of two to five things you want to start doing or get back to doing. Check one item off your list every week. After you have done all the surface level items, then think about digging deeper to attain inner peace. Make that list and start working on those items as well. You will notice a difference in the way you show up in love and in your life. You will be recharged, refreshed, and ready to shine for your spouse, your family, friends, and those in need!

Get rid of fear

The first step to creating an awesome love story involves tackling the one thing that interferes with our goals: fear. Fear is the killer of every dream you have, including your dream relationship. I love how Les Brown explains fear as an acronym. He says "F.E.A.R. is False Evidence Appearing Real." I believe this to be true. Fear will indeed destroy your relationship. It will have you holding on and thinking you can control every situation like questioning why your spouse didn't tell you he was changing plans to hang out with someone else or trying to make your spouse come home after being out of the house longer than you anticipated. Fear and anxiety lead you to worry about the future in unhealthy ways. Your mind obsesses over what could go wrong in your relationship and life, often causing you to miss out on what's going well. More importantly, the things we fear often never come to fruition, but the damage anxiety leaves in its wake is laid out behind us in startling relief.

Fear will have you ready to run away from and give up on everything you have worked hard to achieve in your relationship. Fear will have you thinking things are too painful to deal with. Fear will keep you from opening up and allowing anyone to ever get close to you. It will never let your spouse see the real you without your mask, the mask you show to the world in order to be liked or to fit in. Fear will never let you trust your spouse for the entirety of the relationship, eventually leading to its demise. Fear will stop you from taking action. Fear will keep you uptight and unable to relax leading to many, many health issues. Fear can and will have you thinking you should only stay superficial when it comes to your spouse, not realizing its cripplingly effect on your relationship because we all need that deep emotional connection with our spouse. Fear will stop you from ever reaching that happily ever after feeling. Fear will keep you stuck always trying to avoid being hurt. Fear will halt your growth. Ultimately, fear will destroy every relationship you enter into on a subconscious level.

Let's look at a real-life example. Larry and Jenn had been together for about six months. Jenn believed he would eventually leave her just like all the other men who came before Larry. Even though she was skeptical about the relationship, she tried her best to remain optimistic about the two of them. You see, Jenn's dad walked away from Jenn and her mother when she was

CHAPTER 1

just five years old. There also had been plenty of men to come and go in her years of life. She watched her mother go through many "uncles" (this was what her mom called the men). Jenn also had experienced this on her own since she becamean adult. She did not understand why it seems men only stayed in her life for short periods of time. As a result, Jenn became paranoid every time Larry left the house, whether they had a fight or not. She wondered if this would be the day he left and never returned. Her constant worry about if Larry would leave her started to affect her frame of mind.

Larry would always try to comfort her and soothe her feelings of insecurity. He tried to assure her that he loved her and would be there for her, but he wondered if he was making a mistake by staying around and trying to work this relationship out. Jenn started to accuse him of wanting to leave her. She started making statements about him leaving and never coming back. He would often wonder where all of this was coming from. Jenn would usually tell Larry nothing, or she would stonewall him.

After going through this cycle many times, one fateful day, Jenn decided to face her fears and let Larry in. She let him into her deep world of being scared that he, too, would leave her behind like all the men before him. Before confessing what was happening, Jenn was very afraid that he would leave her after she confessed her fears. She took a deep breath and began. She explained about her dad leaving when she was younger and about all the men that her mom would have her call *uncle* but who never stayed. She further explained how she, too, experienced men leaving her behind like an old pair of dirty sneakers. Jenn explained to Larry how this made her very vulnerable and insecure about every man with whom she became romantically involved. She confessed that she had started to think he would do the same thing to her because they had been having a few misunderstandings recently. She also revealed that she had been waiting for him to leave her for quite some time. Larry sat there and listened to the entire story without interruption. He wanted to hear everything so that he could understand his girlfriend.

Afterwards, Larry thanked her for opening up to him and told Jenn that although he understood her fears, he was not like those other men, so she would have to trust him and see the outcome of things. Jenn agreed to work on this.

It is a good thing Jenn decided to open up to Larry about her fears of him leaving her behind. This could have been a total disaster, ending in a breakup prematurely. Larry understood why she would seem so insecure about him leaving for the day and especially after an argument. Jenn saw the benefits of sharing her story with Larry and started to relax into the relationship each day.

So, how do you get unstuck from your fear? You have to push past the fearful feelings and do the thing that you are afraid of doing! It is simple, but not easy to do in most cases. However, if you push past the fear

CHAPTER 1

and just do it, you will be much more confident in yourself and when the next hurdle comes your way, such as having a tough conversation with your spouse, you will feel the fear and do it anyway! Each time you conquer a fear, the more its power lessens and the more you will see your dreams of creating the relationship you have always wanted come true.

Being fearful can bleed into you not dealing with your baggage. Yes, your baggage! We all have some! Have you worked through everything that has happened to you, including those things you carry around with you from your childhood? Have you sat back and analyzed your last relationship or the one before that or even the one before that? Are you one of those people who jump from relationship to relationship carrying all the things that now hurt you and your chances of having a successful relationship? Do you wonder why you can't have a great relationship or why they keep failing?

Most people do not understand how important this step is. What is baggage? Baggage is anything that you have experienced in life, and now you hold it against your new partner because you constantly put everyone into one box as if what happened to you will happen repeatedly no matter with whom you are in a relationship. Simply stated, baggage is an issue regarding a person's past that can affect their current disposition: addictions, debt, diseases, bad habits, past relationships (romantic or familial), or kids. In this case, I am referring to the things you can get rid of, specifically, the past relationship issues, bad habits, and maybe some debt.

Baggage can be detrimental to your relationship and will surely have it going downhill if you do not or have not dealt with the things that will inevitably hold you back from being the most open, loving, and the best communicator you can be. For example, you had a mom who was abusive, and you keep ending up in these relationships with an abusive partner. Maybe you think this is the way they are showing you love. Maybe you keep ending up with a jerk. You know, the guy who behaves the same way, treats you the same way, and even wears some of the same cologne but has a different face from previous partners. He is plenty of your exes wrapped into one guy and yet you keep attracting him. Why is this? This relates to you not dealing with your baggage and not understanding how worthy you are at this point in your life. You deserve better out of life!

Michelle had to learn this. Michelle's mom left her and her dad when she was just three years old. She had a few memories of her mom living with them, but they were not good memories. Her dad and mom would argue to the point of being abusive to one another, whether verbal or physical. The physical did not happen that often, but they verbally abused each other throughout the relationship. However, she did not understand the abuse back then. What she did understand was that something about those situations did not feel right to her.

CHAPTER 1

One evening, after another fight with her husband, Michelle's mom decided to walk away for good and not look back. She left Michelle and her dad alone, trying to figure out what life was going to be like next. Michelle never forgot how she felt that night and many nights that followed.

Because Michelle had never seen a family therapist or had anyone she could talk to about what happened and how it was not her fault why her mom left, she just kept her feelings bottled up. Because she believed that this was what people do, even when they said they loved you, she knew that her day would come when she would be in love and he would walk away from her, just like her mom had left her dad. Michelle was right! Every man she tried to form a lasting bond with left her in the cold.

You see, Michelle represents many of us who have never dealt with our baggage and yet enter into a new relationship thinking it will be different. She figured she needed to change the guy, the jerk, she was involved with and every guy who followed. Michelle never thought for one second that she was the problem or at least part of her own problem. Most people do not realize that the number one way to be successful in love is to look at yourself and work on yourself first. Ideally, this needs to be done before entering into a relationship, but most of us have that "try, try, try again" mentality believing this is the key to succeeding at this thing we call love. But it is not! Working on yourself requires you to be open, brash and candid about what is holding you back, i.e. your baggage, from having a healthy relationship. Then, once you have this figured out, you have to make it your mission to find ways to get rid of it. Next, ask yourself as many questions as needed to understand so that you no longer go down that destructive path. What makes me unique? Why did that happen to me? What did I hate about that experience? How did that experience affect me? Was it my fault or someone else's? We have to go on a path of self-discovery to find out who we truly are.

You have to rid yourself of that hurt and pain, so that you can open yourself up to love and to truly connect with another person. Find someone you can talk to, whether a therapist, priest, pastor, a great friend, or a Life and Relationship Strategist, like myself. You can create the relationship you have longed for. That healthy relationship is right around the corner when you rid yourself of your fears and deal with your baggage.

What fears are you struggling with or need to let go of? What do you need to talk to your spouse about? Can they help you through this fear? Find time today or this week to get one of your fears addressed and crossed off the list. What steps do you need to take to get rid of your baggage once and for all? After you write them down, the next step is to take action. This will be another notch on your belt as a couple creating intimacy and understanding.

CHAPTER 2

Happiness is your choice

"Once you learn how to create your own happiness, no one can take it from you." ~Robert Tew

Happiness is not something another person can give or provide to you. Happiness is something you must choose on a regular basis. Most of us find a way to put the blame on others for how we are feeling and why we might be responding to things a certain way. You must understand that no one can steal your joy or excitement. You are choosing to let that person or thing influence your emotions. It does not matter what is going on in your relationship, with the kids, on the job, or even when something horrible has occurred. We each have a choice to make if we want to go throughout the day with anger, sadness, craziness, wickedness, and yes, even happiness. We are choosing each and every one of these things. There is nothing you can do about what happens to you, but you do have control over the way you react and behave. You are the designer of your minute, hour, day, week, month and year. Every moment of every day you can choose to be happy, no matter what. We also have the power to consciously choose something else, meaning we can become aware of our feelings, identify what the feelings are, actually feel those feelings, simply relax into those feelings, and finally let those feelings go. Simply release them. Let all of those negative feelings flow away from your body. Feel the lightness that comes along with you letting go.

Let's look at Peter and Paula. Paula came home after a long and horrible day at work and started accusing Peter of not cooking dinner the way she asked him to prepare it. Peter could have chosen to get an attitude and give her a piece of his mind, or he could take a step back, put himself in her shoes, ask a few more questions to get a better picture of what was going on with her and then choose to make her feel better in every way possible; or he could scream right back at her about how long it took him to prepare this meal and how ungrateful she was being.

Choose to be happy at that moment even when the time seems right to lash out at him/her. Choose to turn the negative situation into a positive one while still remaining happy and in a state of euphoria. I am not saying this will be easy, BUT it will totally be worth it, as you will de-escalate things and have a better night without the frustration or bringing your own energy down into that negative space. Take back your power and control!

Peter decided to choose happiness and understand why Paula was being so snappy and irritable toward him. He simply asked, "Honey, what's bothering you?" Paula described how stressful her day was, how all of

CHAPTER 2

her meetings ran over and because of that, she had to start every other meeting late making her rush to complete other tasks. To top things off, her boss was not being the nicest person that day. She had so many deadlines to meet with so little time left over. She explained how she was angry at the way her day went, and that it had nothing to do with him. She immediately apologized for her behavior, and he accepted her apology.

Even with all these things going on in Paula's day, Peter had nothing to do with any of them, and yet he still felt her frustration. Paula did not handle the day very well when it came to her own happiness. No matter how the day unfolds, we have to choose to be happy even in the most stressful situations. We also have to remember that our spouse is not the person who should ever feel our frustrations about someone or something else indirectly.

Being in an intimate relationship with your spouse can sometimes be nerve-racking and you can lose it very easily, not because you are callous or a bully, but because your spouse knows which buttons to push and how to get you to react to things. Also, we care deeply about what they think about us. Sometimes we end up going down the rabbit hole of yelling, shouting, and even name-calling. Do not do this under any circumstances!

You might not think it is a big deal to call your spouse out of their name, like bitch, hoe or asshole, but it truly matters. It matters because the conversation or argument has now gone from a semi-productive fight to one where he or she is not listening at all. Your spouse has started to focus on the blatant disrespect versus the real issue. The second you call your spouse out of their name, another fight has just begun, again, distracting you both from the original issue, leading you further away from a solution. You also do not want to be responsible for making your spouse feel the emotional pain that accompanies the name- calling.

Larry would often call Jill a fat slob. He did not notice or think anything was bad about his words. He figured he was trying to encourage her to lose a few pounds of the extra weight she had put on after the birth of their son, Jacob. Not only did Jill think she was ugly, she also hated that Larry addressed her in such a negative way. Before Jacob was born, Larry often told Jill how beautiful she was, and he could not keep his hands off her. Jill would often think, "My how things had changed after Jacob."

One day, Larry lashed out and called Jill a fat slob. Before Jill realized what had happened, she yelled, screamed, and shouted at the top of her lungs: "I'm sick of you calling me a fat slob, and I will not take this any longer. You can make your own food." Jill then stormed out of the house. She felt hurt, angry, disrespected, and in need of some space. Larry looked around, dumbfounded. He wondered what he had done wrong. Jill never complained about the way he spoke to her before.

Over time, name-calling can lead to depression, anger, anxiety, hostility, dissociation, and decreased marital satisfaction. Marco Iacoboni, author of *Mirroring People,* writes about how our brain is wired to communicate with other brains. The closer and longer the relationship, the stronger the neural connection is between couples. What this means is that over time we contribute to the changes in our partner's brain and they with us. It would follow that if we have positive ways of communicating, it will strengthen the neural pathways that support healthy communication. However, the opposite may also be true. If we get caught in negative cycles of communication with a partner, we will be supporting those pathways as well.

Just because your spouse is acting like an ass, it does not mean you have to outwardly call them that. When you are recounting the details to friends and family later on, you will not get much sympathy because you called him or her out of their name (at least you should not if you are speaking to another emotionally mature adult). They will be able to see the error in your tongue, even if you are not able to. According to Daniel Sonkin, author of *Sticks and Stones Will Break My Bones: Name-calling in Intimate Relationships*, for most people, the urge to spout negative language comes in response to a set of emotions called withdraw emotions. Withdraw emotions are reactions that make us want to pull away or fight with (e.g., the flight or fight response). Withdraw emotions typically arise in response to emotions that feel bad – anger, frustration, fear, sadness and disgust. People usually do not feel the need to put others down when they are feeling happy and satisfied; they do it to express displeasure about a situation. An important point about withdraw emotions is that there is nothing wrong with feeling upset about a situation, event or person.

This does not mean you cannot take up for or defend yourself. You have to be aware of the harm that comes from using this language toward your spouse and how it never ever works out for your benefit or the benefit of the issue. It only further complicates it. The main way to defend yourself is to let your spouse know that he/she is being cold, rude, mean, or thoughtless. See, now you have defended yourself without using harsh words. And you can keep the focus on the original issue. Here are a few ways name-calling can affect your spouse. It:

1. Erodes a Victim's Sense of Self
2. Affects a Victim's Sense of Well-Being
3. Affects mental health
4. Affects physical health
5. Impacts a Person's Identity
6. Opens the Door to Violence
7. Encourages Internal Criticism
8. Impacts Mood

CHAPTER 2

When you start to become angered and want to call your spouse out of his or her name, stop, think if it is really worth the damage it could cause, take a few deep breaths, and finally make a different choice by addressing the issue directly.

What do you do to make sure you are choosing happiness every day? What needs to change to make sure you choose to be happy no matter what? How will you now show up with your spouse in your times of frustration? Why is name calling an irresponsible choice? How will making a different choice before calling your spouse a derogatory name improves your relationship? How do words affect the feelings you have associated with your spouse? How can changing the way you speak to your spouse enrich your love life? What is the one thing you can do each day to choose to be happy on purpose? Now go out and do that thing!

Laugh often

Life can be so tedious and stressful at times. An easy way to take away some of the stressful moments is simply to laugh as often as you can even when times get rough. Laughing will help keep the stress levels at bay because it releases those feel-good hormones--endorphins. These pain-relieving chemicals are created in response to exercise, excitement, pain, spicy food, and love. However, they can help you ignore pain as well. These endorphins interact with the receptors in your brain that reduce your perception of pain. With high endorphin levels, we feel less pain and fewer negative effects of stress. This helps you in your relationship because you never know the kind of day your partner has experienced. Getting your partner to laugh will reduce their stress levels, which allows him or her to open up and talk to you or just relax with you in his or her company.

This is an easy one for Alice. She laughs all the time, but for William this could be an arduous task. It took him being in a relationship,with Alice to learn how to laugh more. He told Alice even his childhood friends said he had lightened up since meeting her. It will take some practice, but he is learning to just relax and not take everything so seriously.

See, laughter helps each of us in the relationship. If laughing is a hard thing for you to do, then practice looking at yourself in the mirror making silly faces; this should help build up your laughter. Any time you get in a hard place in your relationship, stop and do this exercise. This will help you reset. When you return to the conversation, you will be able to express yourself better and actively listen to your partner. Laughing also helps you bond with your partner. You two will be creating memories... happy memories, of each other and the good times in your relationship.

Here are some other benefits to laughter, according to Corey, a Licensed Marriage and Family Therapist, Licensed Professional Counselor and author of the article *The Importance of Laughter in Marriage*:

1. Stimulates the immune system
2. Increases natural painkillers in the blood
3. Decreases systemic inflammation
4. Reduces blood pressure
5. Brings couples closer together
6. Helps keep a relationship fresh

This article also states there are other medical benefits in addition to the ones listed above. Our cardiovascular and respiratory systems benefit more from twenty seconds of robust laughter than from three minutes of exercise on a rowing machine. Through laughter, muscles release tension, and neurochemicals are then released into the bloodstream, creating the same feelings that long-distance joggers experience known as "runner's high".

Studies also show individuals that have a strong sense of humor are less likely to experience burnout and depression and they are more likely to enjoy life in general, including their marriage. Helpguide.org highlights the benefits of laughter as well:

Humor and playful communication strengthens our relationships by triggering positive feelings and fostering emotional connections. When we laugh with one another, a positive bond is created. This bond acts as a strong buffer against stress, disagreements, and disappointment. Laughter is an especially powerful tool for managing conflict and reducing tension when emotions are running high. Whether with romantic partners, friends and family, or coworkers, you can learn to use humor to smooth over disagreements, lower everyone's stress level, and communicate in a way that builds up your relationships rather than breaking them down.

In short, laugh as much as possible with your spouse to have a more enjoyable experience and a long-lasting, happy, fun-filled life together. This includes, but is not limited to, the two of you rolling on the floor laughing, having a dance-off then laughing at the one who can do the silliest stunt or recalling a funny story that happened to you earlier that day.

When is the last time you and your spouse had a long, hard belly laugh? The one where your stomach hurts and abs cringe because there is so much laughter going on? If you are still thinking about it, then create this moment today. These moments are easily created and will help you both relax into each other, strengthening your bond.

CHAPTER 3

Show more love, gratitude and appreciation towards your spouse

"Gratitude is the healthiest of all human emotions. The more you express gratitude for what you have, the more likely you will have even more to express gratitude for." ~Zig Ziglar

Showing your spouse that you love him or her helps you to develop a deeper, intimate and intense connection with him or her. Love is an action word! Do all the things you know your partner will appreciate, smile at, and adore you for. This includes making the bed, putting down the toilet seat, bringing thim or her coffee/tea without asking, noticing if he/she isout of soap and replacing it, bringing flowers, writing poetry, giving him/her little surprises, or cuddling, just to name a few things. Love your spouse the way he/she wants and NEEDS to be loved.

Do you know your spouse's Love Language? This is a sure way to love them the way they need to be loved. If neither of you knows what your Love Language is, then I suggest you go to Google and search for the Love Language quiz. Here's a short recap of the Five Love Languages:

1. Quality Time

2. Receiving Gifts
3. Words of Affirmation
4. Acts of Service (Devotion)
5. Physical Touch

For a deeper meaning of each Love Language, read Gary Chapman's ***The Five Love Languages: How to Express Heartfelt Commitment to Your Mate***. As you see, many are self-explanatory, but the book really gives a deeper meaning to each one and explains why it is so important to love your spouse the way they need to be loved. You can also Google the Love Language quiz to understand which Love Language is most important for you. Ask your spouse to take the quiz, too; then discuss the findings together. Chapman's research found that many couples with broken relationships that started practicing their partner's top three Love Languages improved their relationship exponentially almost overnight. Just by incorporating these simple new changes, the couples' relationships were more loving, and they all felt more understood by their respective spouses. Small, easy changes make all the difference in creating and maintaining a healthy relationship.

Take Mike and Mica for example. Mike's love language was expressed by giving. Every time Mike noticed something he wanted to gift his wife, he bought it without much thought. He knew she would love it, or so he thought. The more Mike bought Mica gifts, the more he noticed her reaction. It was not as

CHAPTER 3

"appreciative" as he believed it ought to be. He was quite perplexed but just attributed her responses to her being tired or rude or the gift probably not being the great gift he figured it would be.

Mica's love language, on the other hand, was Acts of Service. As much as she appreciated the gifts she received from Mike, what would turn her on more was him helping out around the house! Gifts were further down on her list of Love Languages. She often needed help with the household chores and other tasks such as cleaning the basement or changing a light bulb. She thought she expressed this to Mike, but it seemed he hadn't heard her. She needed to figure out another way to communicate this to him so that he understood why this was so important to her without sounding ungrateful for all the lovely gifts she had received. She knew she needed to express her feelings; she also needed to be sensitive to Mike and his efforts of trying to please her.

The next evening, Mica waited until Mike had eaten and was in a good mood and ready to converse with her about her day, one of their many routines of winding down together. Mike explained how his day went and waited to hear about Mica's day. She started the conversation off with the pleasantries: "It was fine. Nothing bad to report." Mica then segued into what was really bothering her. She said, "Mike, I've been thinking about something, but I have no idea how to explain it to you without sounding like I'm being ungrateful." Mike said, "Don't worry about that. What is it?" Mica explained how much she appreciated the gifts he showered her with, but she would feel more loved if he were to help out more, to ask her what she needs help with rather than buying gifts. Mica explained how Acts of Service is her Love Language and that receiving gifts are great, but they are lower on her roster of what makes her feel loved. Mike said he understood and that he would work on it.

As long as Mike holds up his end of the bargain, their relationship will blossom. Each time something needs to be addressed and they discuss how they feel about it, their relationship will flourish because they both will feel heard and understood. Isn't that what we want, to feel heard and understood?

Another thing to keep in mind is making sure you understand how your spouse needs to feel loved. We often show our love to our spouse the way we want to be loved. In Mike and Mica's case, Mike's Love Language is gifts which is why he would shower Mica with them. Now that Mica has explained the importance of Acts of Service in her life, Mike can now love her the way she needs to be loved, not the way he thinks she needs to be loved.

Pay attention to this in your own relationship. Have a conversation about the Five Love Languages to confirm and understand how to properly show love toward your spouse. If you already have had this conversation, then think about the last time you performed your spouse's Love Language. Also, research shows that those men and women that emulate the top three Love Languages expressed by their spouses are the couples that are the happiest in comparison to those that only give and show love only with one or two. So find out and express love with your partner's top three Love Languages and watch how much more alive each of you feel and show love toward one another.

How do you show love to your partner? Do you show love to him or her the way they want to receive it or the way you think they want to receive it? If it has been a while, then do something about it today! Becoming aware of your spouse's needs and not your own will take some practice. You will always feel the love and see how happy you make your spouse by implementing these small but effective changes. The next time you see your spouse's expression change and you wonder what is happening, think about whether or not you are expressing love to him or her the way they need it.

Gratitude determines your attitude

Gratitude! We have heard this word thousands of times but what does gratitude mean? According to the dictionary, "Gratitude is the quality of being thankful; readiness to show appreciation for and to return kindness." An even more helpful definition is from Harvard Medical School which states, "A thankful appreciation for what an individual receives, whether tangible or intangible. With gratitude, people acknowledge the goodness in their lives. . . As a result, gratitude also helps people connect to something larger than themselves as individuals whether to other people, nature, or a higher power."

Showing your gratitude simply means voicing to your spouse and kids, if you have them, how much you appreciate them for doing a certain thing. For instance, your spouse has just brought you a cup of coffee without you having to ask for it. Here is your opportunity to give him or her a bit of praise, just for thinking about you. You could express your gratitude simply because he put down the toilet seat. This is a big one and one he will be happy to hear about. Maybe your child has picked up all of his or her toys without being asked to do so. These are examples of a few moments to give your family praise. When you do show your gratitude for them doing these small things, they will do them more often. For them, it will be more about receiving the praise, but for you, it is a way for them to help you out. They will not realize how much more work they are taking off your hands as a result of you showering your praise on them. I use this in my relationship all the time, and it definitely makes a difference, especially with those never-ending dishes!

Stanley, Misha's husband, grew up in Africa where many traditional women do all the domestic duties including taking out the trash. The men do not lift a finger when it comes to household work. Now that Stanley lived in America with Misha and their daughter, he was learning to help out around the house more. He hated dishes in the sink! They did not bother Misha as

CHAPTER 3

much, so she let them sit there for a day or three. After she was finished with all her chores, working outside the home, caring for their daughter, teaching her, encouraging her, and the like, Misha was dead tired. She was completely pooped most times. So, Misha felt that the dishes could wait another day until she felt like cleaning them. They also did not have a dishwasher, so the dishes were cleaned by her hands or Stanley's.

The first time Misha came home and saw the dishes cleaned and in the drying strainer, she said, "Wow! You did the dishes! Thank you sooooo much." She made a huge deal out of him helping her out. He totally sucked it all up. Misha said, "I am so tired, but I was coming home to do the dishes today." They were sitting in the sink for a few days. He made a joke about him not wanting to see the dishes in the sink for a long period of time, so he helped out.

After that first time, Stanley has helped wash the dishes many times, and each time Misha gave him massive praise. He even has to point it out at times. He wants his "thank yous." He has made that known. By showing and giving him this praise and moment of acknowledgment, Stanley will continue to help out more and more around the house. The key to remember is that Stanley may not help every time, but he will give Misha more relief as the years pass while they are together. He will not realize he is going against his cultural upbringing. He will be doing it to make sure he pleases his lovely wife, Misha, AND because he is looking for that praise over-and-over again.

REIGNITE YOUR RELATIONSHIP BY 7X

You can do this as well. No longer complain about something your spouse is not doing. Wait until he or she does something that you love or can show gratitude toward, then lay it on thick. Be believable as well. Lay it on too thick and it is no longer genuine. Vocally expressing your gratitude lets your spouse know you feel loved and cared for. I know you will see a big difference by acknowledging and showing your gratitude/praise outwardly. It may take a few times before you see any big difference but keep at it, and there will be more simplistic surprises for you to come in the future.

Now, let's move on to verbalizing your appreciation. According to Sheri Stritof, author of ***The Importance of Compliments in Your Marriage***, when you give sincere encouragement and compliments to your spouse, several things are accomplished:

1. Your spouse's self-confidence is increased.
2. Your own self-worth is increased.
3. The friendship between the two of you is strengthened.
4. You are demonstrating your appreciation.
5. You are making your spouse feel cherished and valued.
6. You are focusing on the positive instead of the negative.
7. You are creating an unforgettable moment between you both.

CHAPTER 3

Sometimes we get in the rut of our routines. Because we live with our spouse, it is super easy to overlook the great and amazing things about him or her. When they dress up or look especially handsome, we take this for granted. We even feel entitled to them doing this on a subconscious level.

The key to complimenting your spouse is avoiding those fluffy, buttery compliments where the giver (you) is looking to receive something in return. The best thing about a compliment is that they are always accepted. Paying a compliment will keep you focused on the things you like and cherish about your spouse. When you live with your spouse, it is easy to take him or her for granted and forget about or notice all the big and little things they do on a daily basis to make you happy. These were the things you once acknowledged, raved about, and appreciated. Being appreciated by others is one of the most basic human needs. Giving a compliment will show your appreciation to your spouse.

I remember working with Terry and Teresa. They had been married for 10+ years. The compliments in their relationship had long fizzled out. Teresa would get all dolled up for Terry, but he would not notice. Terry was often preoccupied with other things. The words, "Oh honey! You look beautiful," had long passed. Teresa wondered what it would take to get this feeling of being wanted and adored by Terry back again.

REIGNITE YOUR RELATIONSHIP BY 7X

One day, Teresa decided to have a talk with Terry about her feelings and how she longed for those compliments and why they were so important to her and her feeling attractive to him. Terry did not realize this was a problem. He decided right there that Teresa deserved to feel as though she is needed, special, and loved. He promised to do better.

Giving a compliment also builds the intimacy, physically and mentally. Compliments show how much you respect and pay attention to your spouse. Most importantly, giving a compliment shows that you are making it a point to focus on the good in the relationship. Also, giving a sincere compliment boosts the mood between you and your spouse.

Noticing something you like or smell on your partner means nothing if you never verbalize these things to him or her. This moment to connect with him or her could easily become lost. Compliments are important to give to your spouse because the relationship often becomes stale and complacent, ultimately resulting in taking each other for granted. Also, this can make your spouse believe you are no longer paying them any attention. Verbalizing your thoughts also shows that you are invested in the relationship, and it bolsters your overall communication, one of the key elements to a happy, healthy relationship.

Research has shown that when we complement each other and focus on the positive things about other people (and other things), we shift our attention from a negative mindset to a positive one. The fact is, a compliment is a two-way gift. When you give a compliment to someone else, especially your spouse, a chemical reaction of pleasure takes place in your brain. The same thing happens to the receiver of the compliment. This helps you stay focused on the many, many things you like and love about your spouse, again reinforcing the connection and intimacy.

How will you intentionally show your gratitude toward your spouse? Your child(ren)? Do not let the next opportunity to praise him or her pass you by. Remember, it can be a huge surprise that you are praising him or her about, or it can be a very small, wonderful thing he or she did. Either way, make sure he or she feels the love and appreciation being outwardly expressed toward him/her. Finally, practice giving your spouse one compliment every day. Keep finding what you like about your spouse each day, and build up the number of compliments to five per day. You will notice a shift in your relationship and how much happier you will be with the person you chose to spend your life's journey with.

CHAPTER 4

Be intentional and show respect toward your spouse and relationship

Be intentional to add value to every person you meet everyday. ~John C. Maxwell

Being intentional in your relationship takes practice. By being intentional, your spouse and relationship will thrive and flourish. What does being intentional mean exactly? According to the dictionary, being intentional means done with intention or on purpose; intended. Many people believe that once they find the love of their life, they will stay in love and everything will fall into place, including having a marriage they are proud to be a part of and one they will showcase to the world. Many people date, get engaged and marry without thinking about how their relationship will look five, ten, or even twenty years down the road. It is easy to fall in love but staying in love takes being intentional and maintaining the effort you put forth toward the relationship.

Being intentional means setting relationship goals, actively seeking skills and education to become more effective lovers, and making sure you two have relationship checkups to see if your goals need to be adjusted or if they are being met. Being intentional means paying attention. It means doing things on purpose, not being passive, and not because you have to do these things. You are being intentional because you want to be intentional! You want to see your spouse laugh, have fun, and enjoy life, but not with just anyone, with you! Being intentional means finding out the way your spouse needs to be loved and expressing this love to him or her in that way. This is a way to do the nice things for him or her, but a more effective way is to learn your spouse's Love Language (Refer to Chapter 3)

Finding out how to love your spouse is definitely a way to be intentional and maintain your relationship together. Often times, we love our spouse the way we want to be loved. For instance, take Miguel and Susan. They were a young couple trying to make their marriage work but having a hard time truly connecting with one another. Miguel's Love Language was words of affirmation so he kept showering Susan with praises, such as how great she was, how beautiful she was, how he appreciated her and all she does for him, and how differently his life would be without her being a part of it. He had never asked Susan what she would like him to do to make sure he showed her he loved her with all his heart, the way she wanted. What she really wanted was for Miguel to touch her with affection much more often. Susan loved to hug and cuddle and wanted more of that. Her schedule kept her so busy that these moments were what she longed for many, many evenings and nights.

CHAPTER 4

Here's how Miguel and Susan can be intentional in their relationship to make sure both their needs are being met, which will make and create a happier life together. Susan needs to speak up and tell her husband that although she enjoys his loving, kind words of affirmation, all she really longs for is his manly touch. She also needs to explain why physical touch is so important to her. Miguel will understand why he needs to change his tactics of showing Susan love through encouraging words thereby increasing the chances that Susan's needs will be met. Their level of intimacy will grow just by talking through each of their needs and how to meet them.

What action(s) do you need to take to produce feelings of closeness? How can you intentionally love your spouse other than understanding his or her Love Language? Are you willing to do what it takes to keep the fire burning inside and outside the bedroom? What is the one thing you can do today to show your spouse you love him or her? Okay, now that you have thought about it, go do it! Be intentional. Show your spouse you want the fire to keep burning with him or her by your side.

Give respect

Respect is a word we often hear many men repeatedly say throughout their lifetime and in their relationship. Many men have left their relationships because they felt as though they were not receiving the respect they believed they deserved. According to its definition, respect is described as a feeling of deep admiration for someone or something elicited by their abilities, qualities or achievements.

What I want to focus on here is having mutual respect for one another in the relationship. It is a simple idea. It means you treat your spouse in a thoughtful and courteous way. It means that you avoid treating each other in rude and disrespectful ways, such as name calling, insults, demeaning language, ignoring or avoiding your spouse, or talking to him or her sarcastically. Having mutual respect means viewing the wishes and values of your spouse as worthy and taking them into serious consideration. However, being respectful and showing respect can be a bit difficult at times. These ideas are simple but not easy to implement, especially when your spouse touches a hot button that they know will send you into a frenzy. Now an argument has ensued.

Do not join in or feed into your spouse when they are going down the rabbit hole of bad behavior, i.e. being disrespectful. This will only make the situation worse, and you will have to be the bigger person and apologize to get things back on track. Instead, avoid doing this altogether.

Edith learned this lesson the hard way. Edith was chatting with a group of her girlfriends at a party about how Roger, her fiancé, cannot afford to take care of them, how he is lazy and, to top things off, how he just lost his job. Edith was going on and on about all the things she was frustrated about when it comes to her

CHAPTER 4

fiancé. Talking behind Roger's back was bad enough but even worse, Edith never shared how she felt with Roger.

You can imagine how Roger felt overhearing the woman he loved speak these horrible things about him. He did not understand why she was being so disrespectful toward his name and position as her man. After hearing as much as he could take, Roger burst into the room the women were in and started yelling at his fiancée. Of course, the other women were shocked and surprised. They immediately left the room to give the couple some much-needed privacy.

The screaming and shouting continued for some time. Roger explained his position, why he was so hurt, and why he felt disrespected. He asked Edith why she never shared her feelings with him.

Sensing how hurt Roger really was, Edith became quiet and just listened. She did not want to quarrel or fight with her man. She had no idea she was being disrespectful. She had never thought that sharing her frustrations about him with her friends was a disrespectful thing or that it could be taken in that way. In utter dismay, Edith realized she was a part of the problem. She should have been building her fiancé up versus tearing him down. Therefore, she apologized for being disrespectful.

Here's the thing-- sharing your feelings, both good and bad, with family and friends is a natural thing. However, expressing these feelings should never be at the expense of your spouse feeling unloved and disrespected.

Once the respect starts to get lost, it is harder to recover from the loss, further destroying the relationship. Here's a way to reset the environment by removing the negative energy. Simply tell a joke during an argument or have your spouse laugh at something . . . anything. It will help lighten the mood and let you both temporarily focus on something less important, reducing the stress levels of each party involved. Finally, the couples that practice telling a joke during an argument stay in their relationship longer and are happier versus those that do not do this. Here are a few ways to put your disrespectful ways behind you for good:

1. Stop! Think before you speak. Is this disrespectful or can it be taken as disrespect?

2. How will you feel if he or she says it to you? Will you say this "thing" in front of him or her? Or can you only get away with saying it behind his or her back?

3. Be the example. Do not throw him or her under the bus when your friends start going down the rabbit hole of trashing their spouse. Do not join in. Simply change the subject, walk away, or call them back.

4. Find ways to talk your spouse up, not tear him or her down.

CHAPTER 4

5. Do not use sex as a weapon. This is a no-no. Many men still want sex even after an argument. This is the way they show love toward you and the way they want to stay connected to you.

6. Apologize if it occurs. No exceptions!

Have you been disrespectful to your spouse and not realized it? Have you talked to your friends and family about how horrible or how lazy your spouse is when they are not around? Have you yelled or screamed at them for no reason? Have you taken your frustrations out on him or her? Called him or her a bitch, hoe, slut, cunt, asshole, etcetera? Told him or her how stupid he or she is? All of these are acts of disrespect!

If you find yourself being disrespectful, then correct the behavior and keep moving the relationship forward in a healthy way because being disrespectful will create more distance between you and your spouse. So, stay clear of this behavior at all cost.

CHAPTER 5

Listen as your spouse's friend and do not try to change him or her

"You not only do not have the power to change your spouse you also do not have the mandate or calling to change your spouse." ~Dr. Doug Weiss

Trying to change your spouse is a futile attempt. You have to accept your spouse for who they are right now, at this moment. Trying to change someone who does not think they need to change will be an uphill, frustrating battle.

According to Dr. John Gottman, author of **The Seven Principles for Making Marriage Work**, "People can only change if they feel that they are basically liked and accepted the way they are. When people feel criticized, disliked, and unappreciated, they are unable to change. Instead, they feel under siege and dig in to protect themselves." So if you do not accept and like your spouse the way they are right now, it will be a tough battle trying to persuade them that they NEED to change. A person only changes when they are ready to do so, not when someone else tries to force a change out of him or her.

A great way to get your spouse to change without you nagging him or her about it is to become the change you want your spouse to work towards. You will be the best example because your spouse sees you day in and day out. Your spouse will be able to see how you refrain from doing certain things or acting a certain way. This will force your spouse to raise his or her own standards. They will see that the things that used to bother you about them no longer do. You will stop adding fuel to your spouse's fire, ultimately getting him or her to do just what you want him or her to do . . . change.

Let me be clear. I am not talking about changing your spouse's core essence. I am referring to the changes in his or her behavior, compromising your spouse's behavior in service to the relationship and not changing the fundamentals of who he or she is. Your relationship should serve you; you should not be serving your relationship. Compromises in small doses are the best way to keep the relationship functioning and running smoothly. For example, turning down the TV when your spouse is on the phone is no big deal nor is helping with the chores when you are exhausted. These compromises do not imperil your core needs, wants, or desires. When you start to compromise the essential elements of who you are, the cracks in the foundation of your relationship start to occur.

Scott and Elaine had a tough time working through this issue. Elaine was working on herself. Enjoying the changes that were occurring, she wanted her husband, Scott, to do the same. She wanted him to get on the path of becoming the best version of himself. However, Scott did not see anything wrong

CHAPTER 5

with himself as a person or as her husband. Scott liked coming in and playing golf with his virtual friends, going to the bars and eating junk food.

Elaine, on the other hand, wanted and needed something better out of her routine and boring life. She began with working on her health. She joined a gym and began a workout regimen with the help of a fitness expert. She also started reading more books about spirituality to help her develop a deeper connection with God. She felt she was losing her self-worth and was tired of trying to do things on her own. She needed some divine intervention. She noticed that by making these small changes, she enjoyed being with herself more. She viewed life in a more positive light instead of complaining to her hubby about certain things. She noticed that she would ask for more of what she wanted without feeling guilty. She set about becoming more real with herself about everything, instead of lying to herself about different situations to suit her or the other person. She started a bucket list and was beginning to scratch things off her list. She noticed that she wanted more of these feelings and wanted to bring her hubby along for the ride.

Elaine had a conversation with Scott about her feelings and how she would like for him to come along and join her journey and life's vision. Scott rebutted the idea and decided he wanted nothing to do with this. Elaine decided that she liked this new her and that she would continue the journey even without Scott's support. Several months went by, and Scott noticed how much more alive Elaine was, how she had stopped complaining so much, and how she was being a much better wife than before. After about a year and a half, Scott went to Elaine to ask her if he could join in with this new way of living. He expressed how he liked this new her and wanted to become a new him as well.

You have to work on yourself first. You have to become self-aware. Start looking at yourself and identify your strengths and your weaknesses. Recognize the differences and the things that are unique about yourself. Start accepting these quirks as benefits because they make up the sum total of yourself. If you are a bit of a klutz, do not feel bad. Keep embracing this about you.

If you accept yourself and start to make changes, then chances are high that your spouse will see the changes for the better and want to become a better version of himself or herself as well. Scott, himself, saw the benefits of the changes Elaine decided to make. What is more important, he decided to walk alongside her in this journey. Scott only did this because Elaine took it upon herself to continue even without him by her side. Continuing to grow, separately first then together, is a way for you to change for the better.

Change is inevitable. Period! Especially in a relationship. Change is the only constant. It is the only thing we know will happen. Growth is optional, however. Growing together will be a conscious choice each of you must make to keep the intimacy meaningful and the understanding between you two relevant. Growth by definition is the process of developing or maturing physically, mentally, or spiritually. I mean, if you are not growing with your spouse, then what is the point of staying? Why put yourself in a situation where you are miserable because you want to grow, but your partner wants to remain stagnant? It is nearly impossible to be in a relationship for many years and think you or your spouse will remain the same as he or she was years ago or even months ago. The two of you will grow whether together or apart.

Personal growth is essential for any relationship to develop and become mature, including taking the high road and apologizing to your spouse first. Initiating the talk after an argument is a way to grow with your spouse. It also shows that you are growing, especially if your spouse usually is the one to break the silence first. You are saying to him or her that you can swallow your pride and ego and make sure they are okay, while at the same time, you are trying to understand what the fight was all about and why it happened. What is more important, you are showing him or her that you do care about their feelings. You miss sharing your day, what happened throughout the day with your spouse, and you want to return to this connected state right away.

Another way you can continue on your path of personal growth is to stop procrastinating. By definition, to procrastinate means to delay or postpone action, to put off doing something. Most people do not realize procrastinating is not a character trait; it is a learned habit. Because it is a learned habit, it can be unlearned by getting that project or thing you have been putting off done. Have you always wanted to learn the guitar but have never looked into taking lessons? Now is the time to research local music stores to see which ones give lessons. Maybe you have wanted to learn CPR or cardiopulmonary resuscitation to ensure you can save one of your family members or someone in need. Today is the day to call around to see who is offering classes. Maybe you have dreamed of learning how to speak another language. You know it will make you feel good and, also sound smart. Look into finding local classes, organizations, or ask people you know to help you find a tutor so that you can start on the road to becoming bilingual or trilingual.

Neither of you will stay the same person that you were when you first started dating or got married (if you are married). Both of you will change and hopefully grow. You should be growing as a couple, too, learning from each other and constantly trying to be there for one another in the way that best suits you both.

Continuing to work on oneself is a sure way to be more sympathetic, empathetic, and understanding of yourself and your spouse. You will be able to express yourself much better, and you will also want to share these things with your spouse more effectively and with an open heart. If your spouse is not growing personally on his or her own, then they will not be able to understand you or where you are coming from. You

CHAPTER 5

will start to speak a foreign language to him or her. You two will start to grow apart from one another. Some are even scared to grow for fear that their partner will get upset or eventually leave them behind for an upgrade.

Personal growth is not the adversary in your relationship. Here are a few ways in which personal growth will help your relationship grow stronger even if your spouse is not on board.

1. You become the leader because you have to lead by example.
2. You will be more desirable due to you living life the way you want to live it.
3. You will be able to communicate much better with your spouse.
4. You become more self-aware of your actions and how they affect you and your spouse.

What can you write down today to become more self-aware about? How can you start to become a better person and a better example for your spouse? Will you continue the journey of personal growth without your spouse's support? What's the one thing you can do, starting today, that will help you move in the direction of personal growth? Choose something simple that will be in tune with making it a priority to do, then start there and increase your growth every day. Understand, you will not always get this right, but as long as you are trying, it will make all the difference to the two of you remaining a close unit.

The next two chapters focus on other ways to continue in your personal growth journey which are to continue to have a life outside of your spouse and respect "me time". Both of these are ways to continue to grow separately from your spouse and a way to have something to talk about when you come back together and/or a way for you to teach your spouse something new.

Listen as a Friend, Not Someone Who Needs to Solve the Problem

Being a great listener takes practice, patience, and being purposeful. This is especially important in our love life and with our partner. Listening when your partner needs to vent is completely different from listening to him or her in order to help them solve a problem. Most people listen to respond. Very few people listen so that they can hear exactly what their partner is trying to convey. They are not allowing their partner enough time to complete his or her thoughts, in most cases. Most assume that because their man or woman is sharing this issue with them, it means it is a cry for help. However, this is not always the case. Sometimes, you just have to learn to listen as a friend versus the problem solver. Maybe he or she does not want you to solve the problem; they just simply need to get this issue off their chest in order to move past it. This is where active listening comes into play.

CHAPTER 5

Active listening requires the listener to fully concentrate, understand, respond, and then remember what is being said. It also means actively showing verbal and nonverbal signs of listening, such as eye contact, nodding and smiling, agreeing by saying *Yes or Mmmm hmm*, paraphrasing what they are saying, and asking qualifying questions to encourage your partner to continue expressing their thoughts and feelings. By providing this feedback, the person speaking will feel more at ease and therefore communicate more easily, openly, and honestly. This skill can be learned and developed with practice. It can be difficult to master and will take time and patience to develop. The payoff will be worth you taking the time to develop and master this skill. You will be able to hear what is not being said out loud, come to better conclusions about the situation, and help your partner figure out a way not to be stressed over it because you are helping him or her with a plan of action if they desire your opinion.

Listening as a friend is when you let your partner talk and express all of their thoughts so that he or she feels heard and do not want to withhold any details. Another way to listen as a friend is to use open-ended questions. This is helping your partner get whatever is bothering him or her out in the open to figure it out. An open-ended question is often started with how or what. For example, "How do you feel about . . ." or "Can you tell me more about . . ." Next is body language. Body language is a great way to listen as a friend. This can help your partner feel more comfortable speaking to you about what is worrying him or her. Sit with your arms to your sides and stretched out rather than folded across your chest. Try your very best not to be judgmental toward your partner. This is yet another great way to listen as a friend. Be supportive as possible and keep an open mind about what is being said so that you can help your partner figure out the best solution to his or her problem. Finally, validating your partner is another way to listen as a friend. When your partner is describing a situation and it sounds like he or she is having a difficult time expressing it, it is okay to say, "It sounds like you're having a tough time telling me this. I appreciate you telling me about this. Please continue."

Take Lucy for example. Lucy had a hard time when it came to being a great listener for her boyfriend, Lance. Lance would often try to talk to Lucy about an issue, and Lucy would either try to solve the problem or try to finish his sentences or try to rush Lance to finish the story. Lucy did not see the issue as she was always in a hurry to do other things. She was a busy bee.

Lance shut down and did not speak about his issues as time went on. Lucy wondered, after some time, why Lance no longer expressed his feelings to her about anything. When she asked him, he said she was not a good listener, and she would often try to solve his problem when all he really wanted was her to listen and let him vent about things. So, he decided to hold things in. After Lucy heard this, she was quite upset with herself as she, too, hated when she did not feel heard. She apologized for her behavior and promised to work on being a better listener.

Listen so that your partner knows he or she can count on you to be there for them in a time of need, no matter what. You are also doing this because you love your partner and want to help him or her de-stress from the day, week or month. Your partner also has to do the same thing when your time comes along and you need a listening ear.

Are you a good listener or an automatic problem solver? How can you become a better listener? If you are not a good listener, then try practicing this for one to two minutes at a time; then increase your timeframe slowly. You will be a much better listener, your partner will appreciate you more, and you will hear more than you realize because you are not interrupting. Most importantly, you will be present in the moment. Become your partner's best listening ear and most trusted confidant he or she has in his or her life.

Stop being prideful, get rid of your ego and actively listen

Pride and ego are really great at times, like when you are celebrating a completed project or when you are receiving a reward for a job well done or some other type of recognition. However, pride and ego can kill your relationship quickly. Being prideful and having a magnanimous ego can lead to your partner being resentful, displaying anger and malice toward you.

REIGNITE YOUR RELATIONSHIP BY 7X

Ego causes all types of conflict within your relationship because there is no room for a true connection or communication when pride and ego take precedence. Relationships are all about compromise whereas pride is an assertive stance that does not back down. A destructive relationship is the only one in which ego wins because there is no peace when ego enters into your relationship. I love the following two quotes very much, and they fit here perfectly:

"Whenever you're in conflict with someone, there is one factor that can make the difference between damaging your relationship and deepening it. That factor is the attitude." – William James

"People are lonely because they build walls instead of bridges."
— Joseph F. Newton Men

Sean and Samantha's relationship almost did not survive due to them being prideful and letting their egos get the best of them. Sean was a man who would offend Samantha but never felt as though he needed to apologize for his actions, but he wanted his wife, Samantha, to always apologize whenever she did something offensive to him. Samantha would always take the humble road of apologizing so that they could move the relationship forward, but she was getting tired of always having to take the high road. She wondered if Sean would ever see the error of his ways if she never spoke up.

One day, Sean was being very prideful, rude, and disrespectful. He demanded Samantha turn down the

CHAPTER 5

volume on the television. She did, but he did not feel as though the volume was lowered enough. He decided he was fed up with her and turned the television off without another word. Samantha was very upset and shocked at the same time, as Sean had never done anything like that before. After they exchanged a few not-so-kind words, Samantha realized the error of her ways and addressed Sean. She said, "Sean, I'm sorry for being disrespectful to you, but you cannot run the household like that, as if I am a child. I did not appreciate you turning off the television while I was watching it." Sean immediately got offended and held on to his pride. He told her, in a stern voice, that he had nothing to say to her about the subject and that she needed to go to bed (she was headed that way, anyway).

Treating your spouse as if they are a child is not the key. In doing so, Sean will lose everything he has worked so hard to build by being prideful. Did you notice he did not apologize to his wife or try to work things out?

This time around, Samantha did not want to be the bigger person. She let this issue fester for a few days. She knew she was wrong but did not want Sean to believe what he did was okay. She was adamant about him apologizing and seeing the error in the way he handled things. Samantha decided to just be silent, as if Sean and the relationship with him didn't exist.

After nine days, Sean saw that he was wrong and needed to apologize to Samantha. He knew he needed to make things right in order for the silence to end and for them to get back to loving one another. He knew this would happen after they discussed what happened the other day and why it took a turn for the worse. Getting rid of this type of behavior will not come overnight but over time with practice, you and your spouse can and will live without these two, pride and ego, rearing their ugly heads.

This brings me to another deadly deed that often gets overlooked in a relationship: how we argue with our partner. Research shows that the number one predictor in determining if a couple will last is how they argue. How effectively do you and your partner argue with one another without using criticism, contempt, defensiveness, or stonewalling?

What does arguing effectively really mean? I honestly hate to say "argue" because I do not believe in arguing per se. What I do believe in, however, is effective communication. When you communicate effectively, you will feel better about being around your partner, and this will be a determining factor to decide if you want to stay with your partner long-term. Conflicts are built into each of our relationships. No two people, no matter how well they mesh together, will get along in harmony all the time.

Knowing how to argue is essential to your relationship. There are several keys in overcoming conflict (i.e., an argument), such as (1) being respectful (2) communicating your needs (3) owning your part in the conflict (4) not fighting dirty and (5) taking a step

CHAPTER 5

back from the situation. These keys are required and are essential to having an effective "arguing" session.

There are several other things that I would like to point out. The first thing is that you have to be open and honest about the way you feel during that argument. Second, do not be accusatory. Just talk about how you feel, not how he or she did this or that or "You made me do this because . . ." No. Do not be accusatory; just get your point of view out there. Say "I feel sad because . . ." or "I did not like the way this happened because . . ." Do you see how you would not be pointing the finger? You have to take control of your own emotions. You have to own up to them. You have to own up to your part. Using these "I" statements conveys you are taking ownership of the way you feel versus blaming your partner. Your partner cannot make you do anything! You are the only person who can control your actions. So, do not accuse your partner of something that you did by way of your actions. You did it because that is what you wanted to do. That is the way you know how to handle these sensitive situations. We all have control over the way we respond to something. Respond. Do not react!

Then, think about what you want to say and explore these feelings. Next, visualize how you want to deliver your message. It is not what you say; it is how you say it! It is the delivery of your message that makes all the difference. You can say anything and everything. I wholeheartedly believe that. However, if the way you deliver your message is horrible, then it will not be received in a way that says *please hear my cries of hurt and pain*. Be loving to your partner and be able to say *I'm sorry* and mean that you are really sorry. It is better to be sorry than to be right!

Subsequently, be willing to actively listen to what your partner has to say. Active listening means that you are literally listening to what they have to say. You are not listening to respond. You are listening to take in what your partner is saying; think about how you can understand it a bit better. Reword and repeat the statements back to your partner. This ensures you are clearly understanding what they are trying to convey. When it is your turn to express your feelings, speak in a clear and concise way and deliver your thoughts on how the conversation went downhill. What was it that triggered the conversation for you not to take in the information your partner was delivering to you? Be specific and express your thoughts and needs.

Another thing is to figure out or to offer some suggestions on how to fix this particular thing so that this conversation does not have to be discussed anymore. This conversation, this argument, does not have to be a repetitive thing if you come up with suggestions and, of course, let your partner come up with suggestions, and then discuss which one is the best fit. No one wants to always hear how wrong the/she is. We want to hear that we are doing things right. Here is a way to do that. You suggest something. Your partner suggests something. Then you two come together to see what works best for your relationship.

CHAPTER 5

Another goal is not to yell, scream, curse or belittle each other during an argument. You do not want to go there. You want to stay away from belittling, cursing, demeaning, being disrespectful or being unloving. You will notice a difference in the way you two communicate and how much easier and faster it is for these arguments to go away. This does not mean you are not going to argue anymore, but the way you guys argue or communicate effectively with each other will make a significant difference.

For instance, John had a terrible yelling problem. He yelled at his wife Sarah constantly. She would often shut down, cry, and walk away. She did not understand why John was so abrasive and downright mean to her. She was trying her best with everything. She had tried explaining to him how the yelling made her feel, but he would never listen. One day, Sarah got fed up and gave John a piece of his own medicine. John was shocked at her outburst. She had never felt heard, but today was different. John had to listen to what she had to say. She was heard that day, and that was all she wanted.

Finally, I want you to hear your partner out because they are not trying to attack you personally. They are attacking the situation. Anything they deliver to you does not mean they are personally attacking you, the person. They are attacking the situation because their feelings are hurt and your feelings are hurt, which is why the two of you are now arguing. Overall, the goal of this is to be able to express yourself openly and honestly so that each of you will know exactly how it is or what it is you both need to do to put your pride and ego to rest so that this conversation does not come up anymore.

How will you start to get rid of your prideful behavior? Did you see yourself in any of the above situations or people? How will you put your pride and ego to rest? What are two to three things you can do the next time you recognize that pride or your ego are getting the best of you? Write them down now, so you can remember them when the time comes around again. Rehearse them now so you can apply them later when you need help putting your pride and ego to rest.

CHAPTER 6

Continue to Have a Life Outside of Your Spouse

"You are the storyteller of your own life, and you can create your own legend, or not." ~Isabel Allende

Why should you continue to have a life outside of your spouse? Again, we are talking about your personal journey with growth, so this is a way to continue on that journey. In stating this, do not make your spouse your entire world! Things will get boring and you will be adding unnecessary, and sometimes unknown, stress to your spouse. Continue to have fun with your hobbies, especially the ones your spouse does not like to do. This keeps the relationship fresh because you two will have things to talk about when that question, "How was your day?" arises. Your spouse may not understand everything you are sharing with him/her, but it is a way of reconnecting when the two of you come back together at the end of a long day. You are much sexier when you are speaking about something you are passionate about and, just maybe, you are sharing something new with your spouse. It will help them continue to learn something new as well.

REIGNITE YOUR RELATIONSHIP BY 7X

Having a life outside of your spouse does not mean creating another life without him or her. What it does mean is that you are keeping up with doing all or most of the things that made you happy before you two met or even married. When you are happy and fulfilled, you are a better servant to your relationship and family overall. You are recharged and ready to tackle those tough conversations, clean the house, take the kids to their many school functions, and work a full day. You do not feel deprived or feel like you are losing yourself or becoming someone you do not know nor like.

In addition, having a life outside of your spouse helps you grow emotionally, and you are developing a sense of self. You will not feel as though you have lost yourself when the relationship takes off into full bloom. You will be able to recognize when you need to regulate your emotions and make quick decisions, especially if your spouse is unavailable. This will ensure you are loving yourself. There is no other relationship that is more important than the one you have with yourself, not even the relationship and bond you have with your kid(s). Normally, no other relationship will work if you do not have a good relationship with one's self first. This will also help you figure out what else is important besides your relationship.

Also, what happens when he or she decides to shut you out of their world for a period of time because he or she is mad at you? Are you left feeling lonely? Sad? Heartbroken? Is your day ruined? Keep your own power! Make sure you are still continuing with your hobbies, especially after the relationship has taken off. You love yoga, so continue to go twice a week. Do not cancel your plans because he or she just figured out they want to hang out with you . . . after 10 p.m.

Take Sarah for instance. She loved playing tennis. Before she met Shannon, Sarah would be on the court before her lessons started and would stay after to see if she could hit the ball around even after practice. After Sarah met her boyfriend, Shannon, she began to slowly cancel her lessons and altogether stopped after only three months of dating. Shannon noticed Sarah was starting to become very clingy and started asking for all of his free time because she had done this for him. She whined when she wanted to spend more time with him. Shannon, sensing the pressure of being Sarah's everything, ghosted her. Sarah had no idea what happened or why he stopped calling. As we see in Sarah's case, you cannot make him or any lover your everything. It will never work out in a healthy sense.

So how can you prevent this from happening? Continue to hang out with your friends and family. Continue with all of your lessons and the things that make you happy and keep you interesting. This keeps your spouse attracted to you and you feel as though you are following your heart and even your dreams, making you even sexier in the eyes of your spouse.

REIGNITE YOUR RELATIONSHIP BY 7X

What hobbies and socializing do you need to get back to doing? Call that friend or family member you have not talked to or seen in a while and make plans to meet up to hang out or for a drink in the next week or so. You will feel happier and have that sense of you loving yourself and continuing to live the life you are creating all while in a healthy relationship.

CHAPTER 7

Spend quality time with yourself in addition to your spouse

"An empty lantern provides no light. Self-care is the fuel that allows your light to shine brightly." ~Unknown

"Me time" is essential to any relationship. "Me time" is the time where you need to get away from the relationship, focus on what you like or want to do and not worry about anything or anyone else in that timeframe. The length of the "me time" is and will be different for each person. The timing may not seem like the best, especially when your partner is asking for time away from you and the relationship. Some people need only a few hours while others need a full day or two. It just depends on the individual.

The purpose of this "me time" is for you to get away in a way that makes you feel free. Free from duties and responsibilities! A place where you can think clearly. A time where you focus solely on yourself. Not being a mom. Not being a dad. Not being a wife. Not being a husband. Not being a co-worker. Not even being a friend. Not being anything that does not suit you and what you are expecting out of your time in solitude. You may need to take a bath, and this is considered your "me time". You may love to take long walks. You may love sitting in the park reading a long, interesting book. Your "me time" may be getting away for the weekend. Whatever you choose to do in this time is up to you. It is a way for you to recharge, so that you can come back, ready to take on the family role again and be a loving spouse. One who is prepared to solve any problems that need your immediate attention, to work on that project, or even to help out a friend in need.

Understand that your partner needs this time to recharge, just like you do, away from everybody and everything! Do not, or try not to get offended when they ask for this much-needed time away. Respect that this is a growing opportunity for you. Remember, this is an opportunity for yourself, as well, to do some things for you both. Look at your partner's time away as a blessing. Now you can become selfish again for a short period of time. No catering to him or her. You get to sleep in the bed all alone without them hogging the covers or snoring your ears off. You get to cook or not. The choice is yours! Maybe it is customary for you two to make the bed; well, now you do not have to for an allotted period of time. Make the best out of this time and really enjoy it versus sitting around pouting about you being left alone.

Do not call, text or email them during this timeframe. Allow him or her to enjoy their time without you around. Let them miss you. Trust me, you are on your partner's mind and he or she will call you

CHAPTER 7

when the timing is right. For example, in September 2018, I went to Napa Valley on a girls' trip. My husband kept our (at the time) twenty-one-month-old, and I enjoyed my trip with little to no worries. He did not call to check up on me. He took care of things without me around. I am sure if there was something to figure out, he did it without me. I was the one calling and texting to let him know I had made it to my destination and that I would call him in a few hours. This let him know I was thinking about him, but I also did not want him to worry about my safety being that I had traveled via plane then took a three-hour road trip to get to my final destination.

Having this time away brought us a bit closer, as this was my first time away from our daughter for a significant amount of time. This was his first time being alone with her for a long timeframe as well. All went well and I was grateful for that much-needed "me time". I was recharged and refreshed and ready to jump back into my busy, busy life.

After arriving back home, not only were they both happy to see me, I was happy to see them as well. I felt a sense of belonging once I returned. My husband and I both understand the importance of this time. Neither of us condemns the other for wanting and taking this time away. We both understand the blessing and the honor it is for one another.

When was the last time you took some much-needed "me time"? How do you handle it when your spouse asks for time away from you and maybe from your family? Do you get offended, or are you understanding and cheering him or her on to take this time? If it has been that long and you are still trying to figure out that timeframe, maybe it is time to schedule some much-needed moments to yourself so that you, too, can recharge and come back as the loving, understanding spouse. Taking this "me time" will help you practice self-care and self-love so that you will be able to give more to your relationship in return.

Make Time to Work on the Relationship

Many people assume their relationship will magically happen. There is an assumption you should know what to do for your spouse, he or she should know what to do for you, and you both will know how to please one another. This is usually not the case. Yes, most of us understand the basics, but not too many of us put in the effort to find out what makes our spouse smile, laugh, feel heard, and generally enjoy being with them and around them. Relationships take constant work and care to make sure things are running smoothly. It can be a full-time job at times. It is not the *getting* into a relationship that is the problem. It is the *staying* in the relationship over a long period of time, being happy, and wanting to be there that can be the problem. This is where the "work" comes into play. I do not like to refer to relationships as being "work." What I do believe we must do is be intentional and maintain the relationship, making it better for you and your spouse.

CHAPTER 7

It is hard to maintain a relationship in your busy world when you are constantly being pulled in every direction, and everyone is asking for a piece of your time. You might even be working on a big project, building a business or just wanting some peace and quiet to yourself. Maintaining the relationship means sacrificing that extra thirty minutes each night just to be with your partner without the interruption of the kids or technology. Maintaining the relationship also means making that effort to stay connected with your spouse, such as creating a fun date night or being spontaneous and pulling them toward you for a quick dance-off to your favorite song. It can even be as simple as making sure you two take a walk together just to get out of the house and connect with each other.

For instance, Jim and Jane had been married for over five years. Jane complained about Jim coming home with work and never spending time with her or the kids and even when he did, he was not really there because he was focused on what needed to be done at the office. Jim did not realize how he could be effective and less stressed if he cultivated an environment and schedule he could stick to where his wife and kids would feel as though they were just as important as his work. If Jim took one to two hours to really be there with his family, focus on them and the moment, then he would be more focused and refreshed when he returned to his work.

Jane suggested that he create a schedule where he could spend time with the family after work that he would be willing to stick to and try it out for two weeks. If it needed adjusting, then it could be modified after that two-week period. The next night Jim tried being completely there with his wife and kids. And the next night and the night after that, until the two-week period was over. He realized he was more alive and felt free, happy and energetic. He felt as though he was regaining his connection with his wife and their children. Jim noticed this was so different and life-changing that he vowed to schedule other things in his life to stay on track and to feel more alive and less stressed.

Do not let the annoying moments of being in a relationship affect how you act or react. Have these annoying conversations to make sure you both are on the same page. These are the inevitable things that will occur. Everyone in a relationship hates these times but realize that they are a normal part of the relationship and melding their lives with another person. No one is perfect, which means the relationship is made of two imperfect people that are making an effort to be perfect for one another. Most people understand that spending time with and growing old with your spouse is the best part of living in this world and being in a relationship. God did not create man to be alone! So, do not be in a relationship all alone or make your spouse feel as though he or she is alone in the relationship either.

Making time for the relationship does not have to be this grand gesture every time. It is the small things and moments that make us continue to fall in love with our spouses. It is the time you two started dancing and one of you fell because of having two left feet. Or that time you tried to be romantic and created a picnic in the house, only for Murphy's Law to be around every corner, which is everything that can go wrong, will. It is those times you sit around and reminisce about when you need a gentle reminder of why you love him or her so much.

Making time to work on the relationship also means making time to remember the little details about your partner, the things he or she expressed that they have coming up, something you can ask him or her about later on to let them know you care about what you two discuss and also how they did with that particular thing. Remembering the little things helps maintain the love for the long-term. They also have more significance than the grand gestures. These small gestures can be expressed throughout the day, and they articulate the deep-seated and ongoing love you have for your partner. The little details can include sending a text message stating, "Honey, you've got this! Go knock their socks off." Or remembering to pick up the dry cleaning you know they need before traveling for a work-related trip.

Are you like Jim? Do you need to create a schedule to make sure you are not neglecting the most important people in your life? What fun activity can you schedule and make it a routine so that you feel connected to your spouse and family? After you create this new schedule and plan, make sure you take action and start doing it as soon as possible. What little detail do you remember your partner mentioning that you can acknowledge today to make them feel special and loved?

Spend Quality Time Together

Spending quality time with your spouse is essential for things to continue growing and heading in the direction of increased love toward one another. Many people confuse this with just spending time with their spouse, as in being in the same house but with minimal engagement. Just because both of you are physically there does not mean time spent at the same location is the same as spending quality time together. Most people face issues when they let distractions arise and remain as obstacles within their relationship. The two most common distractions that occur within a relationship are children and technology. Of course, our children are important BUT they cannot be the focus of your relationship, otherwise they will become your entire world, blocking out your spouse even if you do not realize it.

You must remember your children will grow up and leave the nest and you will be left with your spouse, especially if the relationship makes it past the years of child-rearing into the empty nest stage. If it does survive, then the couple must reintroduce themselves to one another, sharing their likes, dislikes, goals, wants and needs. Time never stood still while one or both of you were focusing on the child(ren) or

CHAPTER 7

other things. Both of you were entering into another stage in your life, such as learning new things or aspiring to reach goals you never discussed with your spouse, like going back to school for a better skill. Maybe one of you suppressed your dreams because you wanted to make sure the kids grew up in a two-parent home. Now the kids are gone, and it is time to refocus back on yourself.

You do not want to go through this process. One way to avoid having to reintroduce yourself to your spouse is by making the time to spend quality time with them now. Every day. Spending a few minutes together every day will keep both of you feeling close, heard and understood. Ask inquisitive questions. Why, you ask? Because sometimes you go throughout your day and things cross your mind. You may think about them for a short period of time and move on, but something about it keeps coming up, like a nagging feeling that will not go away. As the day goes on, you forget about these little moments. By the time you make it home to your spouse, that fleeting moment has passed only to be thought about again when you are not around him or her. One fateful day, you are around your spouse when you think of this particular thing again. Now you remember to mention it to your spouse . . . months later. Your spouse is now wondering why he or she is just hearing about this idea now, not knowing you were not trying to hide such details; it just kept slipping your mind. Now your spouse is wondering what else you have not shared with him or her and why.

REIGNITE YOUR RELATIONSHIP BY 7X

Mica and Margaret had to understand this very thing. Mica and Margaret were growing apart ever so slowly that neither one realized what had happened. One day, Margaret awoke and found herself in a room, sleeping separately from Mica, with the children surrounding her. She felt lonely and longed for the touch of her husband. She had no idea how to bring this up without appearing so needy. Of course, their relationship did not start out this way, but as the years passed, Mica and Margaret fell into a routine of her rearing the kids while he worked all day and hung out with his friends in the evening and into the night. By the time Mica would make it home, Margaret and the children would be fast asleep. During Mica's time off, he would be in the house with the family but would never interact with them. He always would say how tired he was. Even when the children were not around, Mica and Margaret would be busy doing things separately. They never made time to talk and reconnect, not even asking how each other was doing. They would be like two ships sailing past one another, just there with little to nothing in common. Margaret realized she had not uttered two words to Mica in months, except for asking him to do a task or pay a bill. Nothing that made him feel special, wanted or needed.

Mica would often wonder where he went wrong in their relationship. He knew he loved his wife but had no idea how to make the relationship better. Things had dragged on for so long like this that years had passed and the humdrum routine had been established. How could they get things back on track?

This is an easy yet terrifying fix because it takes action and being vulnerable with your spouse; no one wants to be rejected. Again, try not to focus on your world for a few minutes each day. Give your spouse your undivided attention. Listen to your spouse without interrupting and take in all his or her points. Ask questions after his or her thoughts are complete. That way your spouse feels as though he or she is able to express themselves fully and you know the what, where, and why before asking. In the case of Mica and Margaret, one of them will have to take the first step. This is where most relationships continue to fall apart. Many people let the fear of rejection stop them from getting out of their rut and creating a healthy relationship. Yes! This will be a hard task to do; however, if Mica or Margaret decides to make the first move, then no matter what, their relationship will turn around, and that first day will be long behind them. They will both feel loved, respected and heard and look happier, feel healthier and younger. These small changes of making an effort to stay connected will pay off as the years pass by. The relationship will grow strong and remain unbreakable. However, it takes spending the time together now before things can mature to this point.

What is your idea of spending quality time? Maybe it is having deep conversations or sleeping in with breakfast in bed. Maybe it is sharing household duties, like washing and folding the laundry. Have you shared this with your spouse? Does he or she know what you do to unwind? When was the last time you two went on a date? Did you notice that you want to just hold his or her hand? Create a list of things you want to do when you intentionally spend time with your spouse. This will help him or her understand your needs. Also, you will help with keeping the guesswork out of your life. With our busy lives, we need simplicity more than ever, so make that list, share it with your spouse and start spending quality time today.

Continue dating

Dating again! Yes! Dating again. Dating is another way to keep the spark alive. It is a way to stay connected, and it is another way to have an excuse to spend alone time with your spouse.

Dating can be fun. It does not have to be that dreaded thing you have to make elaborate plans about. Dating needs to be a day or an evening away from everyone other than your spouse, doing the things you both like to do. This can be uber fun! You and your spouse should take turns making the dates. You want it to be an effort you both make to keep the connection alive and strong. A creative way to do this is to have a jar with date ideas you both love to do and once or twice a month, pick an idea from the jar and do whatever comes out of it. Ideally, you want the dates to be a 50/50 thing, as far as what date ideas are thrown into the jar. This can and will take away some of the

CHAPTER 7

guesswork as to which date to plan for the next outing. It also ensures you will have fun because you know it is a thing you or your spouse want to do, increasing your chances of having a splendid night out. It also gives you something good to look forward to because it breaks up the monotony of your week and month. Do not limit yourself to the ideas you two throw into your jar. Think about things you have been wanting to do, even if it is very simple like staying in and watching a movie or having a picnic indoors. Just make sure they are both your ideas, and this is bound to create a fun night.

Dating your spouse can also increase his/her level of happiness, positive communication and sexual satisfaction. By spending time with your spouse, you can increase these important areas in your relationship simply by making these times special and non-negotiable.

The key to a great date is to make sure you do not administrate your relationship when you go out—do not have conversations about finances, household responsibilities, problems with the kids or sensitive issues. You need to talk about those things but not on your date. Date night is about enjoying each other. However, if these things do come up, then do not beat yourself up. Notice what happens, talk about it (try to keep it short and to the point), then move back into the two of you. Make sure you two are being playful, laughing, reminiscing about good times together, and even flirting with one another. These things will ensure you two are more than likely to have another memorable night together this time around.

Let's explore another couple. Mitchel and Marsha were engaged but noticed that their relationship had become stale and boring. Nothing new and exciting was making either one of them want to get out of the house after a long day's work. Marsha no longer wanted this type of relationship. Besides they were not even married yet. She could not say *"I do"* knowing this was what her future relationship looked like. Therefore, Marsha decided to do something about her boring situation.

She started to ask Mitchel several questions about how they could bring the spice and excitement back into their love life. After going through a list of things, each noticed that they needed to do some of the things that made each of them happy, giving the other person a new experience, in most cases. Marsha would choose the first activity to plan. They chose a date to go out on their first adventure. After some time they reported back that each date got better and better, and they felt much more connected to one another again.

Dating your spouse can protect your relationship from deterioration, it can keep you and your spouse healthier, and you both will be able to manage life's stressors. Finally, dating your spouse can and will keep things new and exciting.

Are you in a rut like Mitchel and Marsha? When was the last date you and your spouse went out on? When was the last fun date you two had? How could

CHAPTER 7

making sure you two have fun with each other make a difference in your connection? How much more intimate could your relationship be? Are you ready and willing to do the work to create your awesome love story?

Consider these questions, create a plan, and then take action. Keeping these thoughts only as ideas will not help your love life. You must take action. Date your spouse, have fun, and continue to laugh just as you two did when you first met.

CHAPTER 8

Discuss these relationship expectations: Finance, religion & children

"When you stop expecting people to be perfect, you can like them for who they are." ~Donald Miller

Ahhh . . . those pesky expectations! This is where many relationships lose their luster. Each party assumes the other partner knows what to do, what to say, and how to make them happy. This is a recipe for disaster! None of us are mind-readers. We cannot expect our partner to know just what to do and how to treat us in that special way, the way WE feel that makes us feel special. Most of us have had plenty of relationships but what WE did for the previous partner may not work to satisfy our current one.

Because each relationship requires different things, you have to put in a bit of effort to find out what your spouse needs and wants. This is easy to do, yet so many people complain to others outside the relationship about what their partner is not doing, not realizing that they are part of the problem. Your partner can act only upon the things they know.

This only takes a few minutes to discuss, and you both will feel as though the other person is really fulfilling your needs. All because the conversations have and continue to take place in order to get a better understanding of what each of you expects from the other to feel special, needed and heard. Anything that you want to happen needs to be discussed. Period. Again, NO ASSUMING! Assuming will only hurt the situation, and then you will have to explain why and what you are mad about. In most cases, your spouse has no idea why you are upset or what they did wrong.

For instance, if you have special dates, such as anniversaries, birthdates, Christmas, etcetera, that are important to you, then make sure you express this and the importance of each date to your spouse. I found that explaining the "why" behind the significance each date is special makes my spouse remember much better, increasing the odds of us having an amazing day when this date arrives. Remember each person is raised in a different household, which means what is special in their childhood home may be different from what is special in yours. Your spouse may not know your preference of keeping the butter in the refrigerator versus on the counter. He or she may not know how important it is for you two to wake up early to greet the family while on a vacation. Or your partner may not realize why you hate it when he or she drives really fast.

Keith and Kayla are working on expectations in their relationship. Keith just expected Kayla to know she should not to use her credit card for every little thing she purchases. Keith grew up in a household where you would use the credit card only when

CHAPTER 8

absolutely necessary, meaning only in emergency situations. Kayla, on the other hand, grew up in a household where you spent the money when it was available.

As a result, seeing the credit card statement one day sent Keith into a real frenzy. Kayla had no idea what he was so angry about. After all that yelling, Keith explained the value of a dollar and how credit cards kept people in debt and how the interest rates were designed to keep them continually in debt. He also explained how using cash was better unless there was no other choice to make sure he or she purchases the necessities, not items for short-term gratification. Kayla listened intently as she had never heard of this idea before. She explained to Keith that she would work on improving her spending habits, but he also would have to help her with the temptation of irresponsible spending. As long as Keith and Kayla discuss the nuances they each have and the unwritten rules within their relationship, every issue can be resolved and broken down so that both parties understand the other person's point of view.

Discuss things when your spouse speaks to you in a not-so-kind way. Let him or her know why your feelings are hurt and why they should not speak to you in that manner. Discuss how the children will be raised. Discuss how many dates you two will make happen and who will plan them during each month. Discuss the things that are bothering you about your spouse. Discuss large purchases, such as a car, boat, TV or washer/dryer. Discuss if you two will have joint accounts or not. You get the picture: discuss EVERYTHING! This ensures you two are on the same page about most things and this decreases the chances of unnecessary arguments occurring in the future. Overall, make this the relationship that fits best for the two of you.

Here's another example. Zara's birthday was just around the corner. She was super excited to see what Hitesch, her fiancée, had in store for her later that evening. Zara was home getting dolled up for her man and eager to see what the night would bring. Just then, Zara heard the front door open. "It must be my love," she thought.

When Hitesch walked through the door, he immediately made a B-line to the couch. He did not walk to the back where Zara was. He did not greet her let alone notice how beautiful she looked. As he began to close his eyes and relax on their couch, Zara burst into the room with a playful laugh. She gave him a deep hug as he just lay on the couch like a bump on a log. When Hitesch finally opened his eyes, he wondered what the fuss was all about. He looked at Zara and asked her, "Why are you so dressed up? Where are you going?" Zara replied with disgust in her voice, "It's my birthday. Don't you remember? I guess we aren't going anywhere special? I can't believe you forgot my birthday! How could you be so selfish and so self-absorbed? This is totally unacceptable! You can be such a jerk sometimes!" Then Zara burst into tears, sobbing

CHAPTER 8

loudly, and left the room. Can you feel the tension rising here? Name-calling never helps the situation. It only adds to the problem.

Hitesch had completely forgotten all about Zara's birthday. He did not have anything planned. No gifts. Nothing special at all. Trying to save the moment, he approached Zara and told her he was very sorry about forgetting about her birthday. He then asked, "How can I make this up to you?" Zara took this opportunity to explain to Hitesch why her birthday was so important. She grew up in a family where they made a big deal out of that special day. She wanted to carry that tradition on in her own life with her own family. Zara also did not want her birthday to be wasted any longer. She immediately apologized for calling him a jerk and then said, "Let's go salsa dancing. I want to dance the night away, having a great time filled with laughter and with you."

Do you see how easy it was to fix this issue? Hitesch took responsibility and owned up to his mistake of forgetting about her birthday, and Zara apologized for her comments as well. If he would have lied and tried to play things off, then this conversation could have ended much differently. Zara would have seen through his lies and would have felt disappointed, lied to, and unloved. Also, there would have been another argument to deal with: Hitesch's lying and not taking responsibility for forgetting.

We all are human, and we make mistakes. Not owning up to your mistakes will create even more problems within your relationship. Do not do the things you know will hurt your spouse on purpose. When you do hurt his or her feelings, however, just take ownership of that. Apologize and get back to the fun, laughter and creating a relationship both of you will be happy being a part of. Do not let these things linger and start to fester.

Do not succumb to the pressures of making your relationship live up to the one he or she previously had, even if there are cultural differences. Do not take on their culture 100%. This is your relationship. Not your parents'. Not your friends'. Not your pastor's. Build the one both of you will enjoy!

Being in a romantic relationship is all about growth. It is not easy to say that you messed up or you were wrong or you forgot a special day. Discussing as many of these topics when things get off-course, or even before they get off-course, will help you both understand what the expectations are for your relationship and for each other while in this relationship. These conversations show that you two not only love yourselves but you also love one another and want the best relationship you ever could have imagined.

An uncommon area of stress we bring to our relationship is not having the difficult conversations. Most people shy away from these for fear of how their partner will handle the conversation. Usually, this results from how the other person fights, which is mostly below the belt. Your partner brings up sensitive

CHAPTER 8

information you shared with him or her during a non-conflict moment, and they use this information against you, saying it in a negative, derogatory manner. Or maybe, your spouse throws temper tantrums, engages in name-calling or acts emotionally unstable.

Avoiding or delaying these tough conversations can and will hurt your relationship. Not addressing issues when they arise is always the cause of long-term angst, disengagement and disappointment, and they also never receive the chance to be resolved. Additionally, these stories will start to play over and over in your mind only adding to the problem, and the people in the story, your spouse in this case, increasingly becomes the villain in your eyes.

If you want to avoid seeing your spouse in a negative light, then discuss that fight that went really bad a few nights ago. This is the type of conversation that will force you to tuck your tail and go say *I'm sorry*. Explain why the conversation turned into a fight, why you did not feel heard, and find a solution to the problem. Also, be willing to hear why and where it went wrong for your spouse as well. Why did he or she get upset, why did the conversation take a turn for the worse, and how you can do better as a friend and listener?

This small act of resolving any and all conflicts EARLIER versus LATER will keep both of you connected. You both will feel heard and understood. You will recognize he or she as your teammate. Most of all, it will keep the temptation of cheating or relying on another person outside of your relationship down to a minimum. This breakdown in communication with your spouse is a way to make or break the foundation of your relationship over time. Many people lose their spouse to an outsider because over time this breakdown keeps occurring over different issues or even the same issue, and they allow the distance created from not resolving this issue to interfere with staying connected, making an effort to check in, and making sure the relationship is thriving versus the couple constantly in a state of brokenness, anger, and not speaking for days on end.

According to Focus on the Family, ***"Afraid to Communicate with Spouse About Sensitive Issues"***, whatever your situation, there will always be some topics that are trickier to address with your spouse than with others. Even in the happiest marriages, issues like in-laws, finance, sex, major purchases or holiday traditions can quickly shake things up. Handling these matters can be difficult, but it is not impossible. The important thing is to stay away from the twin errors of 1) avoiding conflict at any cost and 2) escalating conflict into unmanageable chaos. You need to find ways to talk about your concerns calmly, rationally, and constructively.

It is helpful to choose battles wisely and to distinguish between petty issues and important ones. Petty by definition means not important and not worth giving attention to; complaining too much about things that are not important. In contrast, important by

CHAPTER 8

definition means of great significance or value; likely to have a profound effect on success, survival or well-being. For example, having a blowout over the cap not being put back on the toothpaste is a petty issue while discussing whether or not you two want to bring a child or children into this world and your relationship is of more importance. This topic should be given a significant amount of time for discussion to ensure both parties present their opinions. Notice how I did not say yell, scream, or bicker over. Many experts point out that bickering can lead to the demise of a relationship. It is like a chronic warfare that erodes the quality of a relationship.

Let's explore another example. Raymond and Rayé were the perfect couple. They would travel together without so much as a hiccup between the two, until they visited Rayé's family for the holidays. Rayé was up with the family early, whereas Raymond decided he would sleep in. When Rayé went to see what was taking Raymond so long to come and eat with her family, she noticed he was still sound asleep.

Rayé immediately became enraged screaming that Raymond was being disrespectful to her and her family by not coming to fellowship with them. Raymond was dumbfounded. He wondered what the big deal was as he wiped the sleep out of his eyes trying to understand why Rayé was yelling. He was just trying to catch up on some much-needed rest after a long plane ride and travel day. Rayé had never expressed how important it was to her that Raymond come and fellowship with the family before they made it to her family's home.

Even though this was a simple example, Rayé needed to express the importance of fellowshipping with her family beforehand, that way Raymond would not have made this mistake unknowingly and he would have understood how important things like this were for Rayé. This was a tough conversation to have because they never had such an issue come between them before.

Here are some things to think about before you approach those tough conversations:

1. Consider the expected outcome of the issue being addressed.
2. Be specific about what you want.
3. Acknowledge the difficulty of having this conversation.
4. Think about what you want to say and how you want to say it.
5. Have this conversation at a good time and place.
6. Give up the NEED to be right.
7. Stay as positive as possible.
8. Stay focused on the problem.
9. Actively listen to your spouse without interrupting.

10. Take a time-out if you must.

11. Know that this conversation can have a part 1 and part 2.

12. Do not pressure your spouse to keep talking about the issue if he or she needs to take a break and come back to it later.

What expectations do you need to address that constantly arise in your relationship that bother the heck out of you? Plan to have a talk with your spouse about one or two of them this week. Continue to do this until you have addressed everything you can think of. When a new issue arises, share this with your spouse as soon as possible to ensure you two are on the same page of the same book at the same time. You want to be realistic but also have many, many conversations.

Other relationship expectations that should be considered for discussion, ideally, before you two walk down the aisle are: finance, religion and children. The next chapter discusses each one in detail.

Finance, religion and children

Finance, religion and children are the big three factors that trigger divorce most often. These things need to be discussed, especially if you are in a long-term relationship and ideally before your marriage as some do not discuss these things before they get married. So, if you are in a relationship and you have not discussed these things, then this is the week that you really need to pay attention and take action.

Let's talk about the **finance** first. Nowadays, it comes down to the question, or at least it should not matter who is bringing home the bacon per se, who is bringing home the majority of the money? That should not matter when it comes to your relationship. You guys have to figure out a system, a good system, in order for this thing not to become an issue within your relationship. It should not matter who is making the most money because if you really think about it, it is for the benefit of the household. It is for the benefit of the family. It is for the benefit of the children. So, it is your money, even if it is coming in two separate accounts or in two separate names. It is both of your money.

According to Om Paramapoonya, *"How Does Money Affect a Relationship?"*, a Texas Tech University research study suggests that economic hardship evidently has negative effects on marriages. Couples with extreme financial stress tend to have lower levels of satisfaction in their relationships. Emotionally strained by their financial struggle, some people become more hostile, irritable or uncommunicative toward their spouse. Many couples even point fingers at the other for their financial downfall.

Just imagine how many fights can be avoided by having a few conversations to see where your partner is on the topic. These conversations are tough conversations to have but will make a world of

CHAPTER 8

difference in your relationship. They will bring you two closer or show maybe it is time to reevaluate where you both stand on the matter. Make having these talks a priority. This ensures you understand the other person's attitude toward money.

A few things to consider while having your finance conversation and also throughout your relationship:

1. Do not keep separate bank accounts. This lays the groundwork for financial problems later on.

2. Do not think about your salary differences. Focus on your money as a whole. If you are married, this is mentioned in your vows... Two become one.

3. It is easier to commit financial unfaithfulness when finances are separate. You and your spouse can spend your money as each sees fit or maybe have loads of money the other does not know anything about. Recommit your shared goals and remember why you are doing it. Because you two are one!

4. Do not let your expectations get the best of you. Do not let unrealistic expectations pave the way for problems and discord.

5. How do you start to get rid of you and your partner's debt? Come up with a plan and then start working on it.

Moving on to **religion**. Religion is another big topic that can tear down the foundation of a relationship. Have you discussed religion with your partner? This topic can be a deal breaker for many people. You should discuss religion even if the two of you do not have children, but especially if you have them. One parent may want to raise the children this way and the other parent may want to raise the children another way. Or are you two going to throw it to the wayside? Are you two going to practice separately? Are you going to try to find a medium where you two can practice together and "sort of" come up with your own religion? Will the children be able to decide or be forced one way or the other? What are you going to do? Do not avoid talking about this subject or think it will go away. You need to know what your partner feels about religion, in general. Maybe they are atheist; maybe they are agnostic. Will that make a difference to you? Also, be aware of your partner's personal beliefs about other religions. Would you accept their religious value system if it does not go hand-in-hand with your own?

A strong religious foundation can sustain relationships through dark periods, such as the aftermath of an affair. Couples believing their union is sanctified by God seem to have more success than other pairings in overcoming many difficult situations. Brad Wilcox, an analyst on minority couples and religion, says, "The best religious predictor of being happy in a relationship is praying together as a couple."

CHAPTER 8

Christopher Ellison, a professor of sociology at the University of Texas at San Antonio, says, "Couples who believe in sanctification share a sense of purpose that goes beyond shared hobbies, self-interest, and procreation. The couples believe God has a mission for their marriage and perhaps even brought them together." In short, sharing the same religious beliefs makes it easier to practice them and incorporate them into your relationship.

According to the Pew Research Center, people in religiously mixed marriages are less religious than their counterparts who are married to spouses that share the same faith. They attend religious services less often, pray less frequently, and tend to believe in God with absolute certainty less often. They also discuss religious matters with their spouse less frequently than those that are religiously matched. Now that you can see the importance of having the conversation about religion, make sure you discuss this topic when needed and as often as it is needed so you both can realize the needs of one another.

Finally, let's discuss the **children**. Having a child or children is another big topic to discuss. Have you guys spoken about how many children you want if you do not have children now? And if you do have children, does your partner, or even yourself, want to have more? Have you guys discussed what happens if you cannot conceive together? Will you stay together? Will you two decide to adopt? Will both of you be on the same page?

What if something happens? For instance, you guys have a child and something happens to the child, as in the child becomes severely ill or passes away suddenly? Have you thought about it? Have you guys spoken about this? Yes, I know this is kind of morbid, but I address this topic because there is a high probability of the relationship not lasting if a child is to die. Equally as important, I am bringing these things to the surface so that you can understand where I am coming from and why these really sensitive subjects need to be discussed versus waiting until something "bad" does happen and then wondering, "What next?" This way you already have a plan in place if it is needed.

According to Matthew D. Johnson, author of ***"Have children? Here's how kids ruin your romantic relationship"***, for around thirty years, researchers have studied how having children affects a marriage, and the results are conclusive: the relationship between spouses suffer once kids come along.

Comparing couples with and without children, researchers have found that the rate of the decline in relationship satisfaction is nearly twice as steep for couples that have children than for childless couples. In the event a pregnancy is unplanned, the parents experience even greater negative effects in their relationship.

After children enter the picture, things change drastically. Days are gone with the sexy texts. The texts now read like a grocery list of things you or the children need. The relationship is more business-like than ever before. There are more talks about the needs of the children than talks about what each of you need. In addition, there are many things lacking after the children arrive, like sex, money and time. No time for each other, at least not like before. Clearly, this is not what you pictured. Here are a few tips to get things back on track:

1. **Chores:** Post a list of daily chores on the refrigerator or a chalkboard and switch responsibilities each week. This ensures everyone knows who is doing what. Discussion over with before it starts!

2. **Parenting Styles:** Let each other parent the way you want to, within reason. Do not get upset if your spouse allows the child to nap wherever they lie instead of in the crib or bed. Discuss the way you two will handle how much the pacifier will be used, especially in times of a distressed baby. What about sleep time at night? If the baby is crying, will there be co-sleeping, sleep training, etcetera? Again, discuss as much as possible to avoid the arguments and to increase relationship satisfaction.

3. **Sex:** Get back in the mood for it! Plan for it! I know it does not sound sexy to plan, but it will help to increase your bond with your spouse, and it will help relieve some stress. Go on a date to increase the mood and chances of sex

occurring. Also, make sure your room is baby free, no baby and no toys, at night to increase the chance of sex happening again.

4. **Couples Time:** Even though you two are together, there are extra people hanging around as well. You were once a twosome, and now it is a family affair. Schedule some time to spend one-on-one, dates plus brief meetings, to discuss family issues. These include buying new children's items, doctor's appointments, and baby-care.

5. **Grandparents:** Having others around to help out is great, but make sure they know the boundaries before bombarding you and your spouse with their plans and how they can "help" you two out. Mothers and mothers-in-law have a way of coming in and trying to take over because they have had children and they think they know what is best, taking the control away from you and your spouse. This does not have to be the case if you let them know how things will work before they arrive to "help". Discuss with each other how you will go about telling them.

Give these topics some thought and then openly discuss them with your partner. Listen to one another. Go into the conversation with an open mind. Be honest if their answers do not match up to your own. Ask as many of the above questions and more. This ensures you know exactly where your partner is and what they deem as important. You two also will know where the compromise needs to happen and if this is something you two can work through.

You want to be realistic but also have many, many conversations. Is it a deal breaker if you do not have children? Is it a deal breaker if, for some reason, you two cannot come to an agreement about your finances? Is it a deal breaker if you guys are not on the same page when it comes to the religious aspect? Know what you want. Know what your partner wants. Then build your relationship together as one, with or without children.

CHAPTER 9

Do Not Focus on Your Partner's Negative Characteristics

"The very act of accepting responsibility short-circuits and cancels out any negative emotions you may be experiencing." ~ Brian Tracy

Focusing on the negative things you find or see in your partner will only make you start to despise, hate or even wish you were not in a relationship with him or her. You will hate coming home to him or her, and eventually, you will hate being intimate with him or her.

According to Maureen Werrbach, author of ***Why You Need to Stay Positive About Your Partner (And Your Relationship) If You Want Love That Lasts***, people see the overarching view of their partners and relationships through either a positive or negative lens: Positive Sentiment Override (PSO) or Positive Perspective or Negative Sentiment Override or Negative Perspective (NSO). Positive Sentiment Override (PSO) or Positive Perspective is something that couples can work on every day. Having a Positive Perspective of your partner and your relationship helps solve problems during a conflict more effectively, make more repair attempts (an action or statement that aims at reducing escalating conflict), and generally see your partner in a more positive light. Negative Sentiment Override (NSO) or Negative Perspective, on the other hand, distorts your view of your partner to the point where positive or neutral experiences are perceived as negative. Couples in the Negative Perspective do not give one another the benefit of the doubt.

You must make it a point to focus on what you love and like about your spouse and your relationship. Be more accepting and forgiving of your spouse's shortcomings. We all have things that drive us crazy about our spouse. You are no different! Focusing on the positive is a learned behavior for most of us. Our society thrives off of negativity; it is no wonder we hardly see the positive! You must make it a point to find and drink the lemonade when life gives you lemons, or your spouse, in this case. Laugh out loud! Seriously, making it a point where you understand your spouse's intentions when he or she does a certain thing that drives you wild will turn those feelings of disgust or dislike around. For example, my husband likes to scrape the spoon across his teeth when he is eating. This used to drive me bananas! One day, I was irritated and got fed up (he did not know this), so I asked in my most polite voice, "Why do you scrape the spoon across your teeth while eating?" He stated, without skipping a beat, "I like to hear the sound." Well, what do you know? I thought he did not realize he did this, or maybe he was being a jerk because he knew it drove me crazy. Turned out it had nothing to do with me or my thoughts or feelings. Now when he does this, I am

CHAPTER 9

less annoyed by it. Soon enough, I will hardly recognize this *offense* at all. You see, once you get an understanding of why something is occurring, it does not bother or annoy you as much.

When you feel a negative response entering into your mind, stop immediately once you recognize it. Question why you are having those thoughts. Then force yourself to think of and focus on something positive about your spouse. Again, this takes practice but the more you commit yourself to see the wonderful side of your spouse, the easier your relationship will become. You will be happier to be in such a relationship. You will start to wonder how you got so lucky to find such a wonderful man or woman. You will be happy when they arrive and slightly sad when they have to leave your side. The romance within the relationship will start to pick back up as well. You will long for his or her touch again as you did when the two of you were younger, like two teenagers that cannot keep their hands to themselves.

Keep reminding yourself how thankful you are to have such a great spouse. Keep focusing on feeding the good in your relationship. Focus on what is going right versus what is going wrong. Research shows that couples who work on growing the good in their relationships tend to have stronger and more satisfying unions than those that predominantly focus on fixing problems, according to Jaimie Mackey, author of ***How to Strengthen Your Relationship with Positive Psychology.*** By focusing on what you are thankful for

REIGNITE YOUR RELATIONSHIP BY 7X

and love about your spouse, the two of you are building long-term love. Here are a few ways to make sure you are being more positive in life and love:

1. Cultivate your mindfulness skills.
2. Change your attitude by changing your thoughts.
3. Change how you respond to things, annoyances, and the like.
4. Focus on making the present moment the very best and most enjoyable.
5. Present your spouse with positive alternatives.
6. Say thank you for the little things.
7. Practice honesty, even when you are ashamed.
8. Be mindful about how you say what you need to say.
9. Recognize the ebb-and-flow in your relationship.
10. Be kind, even when you do not want to or think your spouse deserves this kindness.

What is something great about your spouse you can focus on to help you see the positive side of him or her? How can learning to stay positive make an impact on your relationship? How will your love life turn around with a consistent focus on the good in your spouse? What are the top five things that will be your go-to thoughts when you need to see and focus on the good in your spouse? What are the top five things you love about your relationship that you will start focusing on to snap you out of focusing on the negative? Learning, practicing and repeating these steps, when needed, will keep you focused on the positive you love about your spouse while keeping those negative feeling at bay and of less importance.

CHAPTER 10

Keep God First

"Remember to always put God first in your relationship, marriage & your home. Because where there is Christ your foundation will always remain solid."
~Anonymous

This final chapter is not one that will apply to everyone who reads this book. However, this concept is something I feel strongly about and the one I feel has helped me persevere through many trials and tribulations throughout my life.

Here is a question I'd like to ask you: who are you seeking guidance from? Think about this for a moment because most of us seek guidance from our friends and family. We have a tendency to put God on the back burner until we NEED him. Until there is no one and then we turn to God. In fact, God should be the very first person that we turn to. I want to quote a few scriptures to you:

Psalms 25:5 (from the NKJ version): "Lead me in thy truth and teach me for thou art the God of my salvation on thee do I wait all the day."

Proverbs 10:17: "He is the way of life that keepeth instruction; but he that refuseth reproof erreth."

Psalms 32:6-8: "6. For this shall every one that is godly pray unto thee in a time when thou mayest be found: surely in the floods of great waters, they shall not come nigh unto him. 7. Thou art my hiding place; thou shalt preserve me from trouble; thou shalt compass me about with songs of deliverance. Shelah. 8. I will instruct thee and teach thee in the way which thou shalt go: I will guide thee with mine eye."

These are very powerful scriptures. They have helped me focus on who I should be praying to and who I should be seeking my guidance from, which is the Lord from above. Not my friends, nor my family.

Now, I am not condemning you for sharing your concerns with your family or friends. However, I am asking you to focus on God first whenever you have an issue. Here are a few tips to get you focused back on God.

1. PRAY, PRAY, PRAY, PRAY, PRAY, PRAY and PRAY some more!

Be very specific in your prayers and pray about everything. It does not matter how minute it is to you. Pray and seek guidance from the Lord up above. He is the only one who can help you get in the right state of mind. Think about this, once you start talking to your friends and family about a particular issue, most of the time they lead you toward the negative or down a path of destruction. It is not usually the help you need.

2. It makes you feel better.

When I attend church services, there is something special about being with other worshipers. I feel the Holy Spirit amongst us. When I have an issue, I pray

CHAPTER 10

about it in the church, and then I leave it there at the altar with God. I walk away feeling as though God has heard my plea and has taken it on for me. All my stress and tension has disappeared.

3. It is where you get the most focused.

You are sitting there in your quiet room or in service, your eyes are closed or maybe they are open, but you are very relaxed. You entered with a very tense situation, and you needed to get some things off your chest. Then you pray, "Lord, help me! Please just help me!" At the end of your prayer, you breathe a sigh of relief. When you are silent and quiet, you can hear God's voice. You can understand his guidance. Many of us are so distracted in this busy world that we cannot hear God's voice nor His instructions.

4. You feel relieved and a weight has been lifted off your shoulders.

Ever wonder why you feel so much lighter? All that dead weight has been removed from yourself and laid down for God to take over. It makes you feel so much better! You see, you are supposed to bring your burdens to God. Bring your burdens to Him and leave them in His hands. Unfortunately, we believe that we have to fight the battle. You must remember the battle is not yours. The battle is not yours! Even right now in your relationship, this is not your battle.

5. Remember your timing is not God's timing.

REIGNITE YOUR RELATIONSHIP BY 7X

It is not your timing. It is God's time. God's timing is always perfect. We always feel like we want to rush things which usually gets us in trouble when we try to take things into our own hands.

I want you to focus on God. Take your burdens to God. Pray about everything you do. When you do pray, make sure your prayers are very, very detailed.

You must get every area of your life in order. Your spirituality is no different because when one thing is out of line, most things are out of line! If your emotional state is out of order, your physical and spiritual states are out of order. Most things are in disarray. You must get everything back into alignment.

If you need to get closer to God, like most of us do, then set some time aside to start reading your Bible. Set some time aside to start listening to some inspirational messages, maybe on YouTube, Google or Vimeo. It even could be a local channel on your television. Of course, you can go to the House of God. Take some time for you to get focused on God. Once you get refocused on God, things will start to align once again because God wants us dependent on Him. God is a jealous God.

I would like to share a personal story before I go. I absolutely got focused on God myself. I started to read my Bible from cover to cover. I had read most of it, skipping a few "books" in the Old Testament. Then I stopped. My point is when I did stop reading my Bible and stopped focusing on God, things started to go back the way that they were in disarray. When I became

CHAPTER 10

realigned, centered again and refocused on God, His perfect plan and Him helping me out in my life, everything started to line back up. Once I got in line with what God wanted and where He wanted me to be, things started to fall into place. Even in my current relationship, everything started to fall into place.

When was the last time you prayed for yourself? Your partner? Your family? When was the last time you prayed as a family? With your partner? If you are still thinking about it, then do it today! The rewards are breathtaking. You will be more joyous, free from unnecessary stresses, happier and ready to fulfill your destiny within your relationship and share your gifts with the world.

About the Author

Marshaun Olaniyan is a certified Life & Relationship Strategist, a Keynote Speaker, Content Creator and the author of *Reignite Your Relationship by 7x: So you can get back to making love and enjoying one your spouse*. All of her content is geared toward creating healthy romantic relationships.

After Marshaun's first marriage dissolved, she kept wondering--- *Why?* So many *Why* questions swirled around in her head. She re-entered the dating scene only to find each of those relationships crumbling. After going through this cycle of jumping from one relationship to another, she decided to take control of her life and her relationship destiny. She started to educate herself on who she was as a woman and what she wanted from herself first and then from a relationship. She learned, unapologetically, how to show up as her authentic self within her life and her relationship. But Marshaun didn't stop there! Marshaun decided to research men and find out how they think, what they like and do not like, and how they want to be treated while being in a relationship with a woman. She also interviewed her exes to hear their side of the story

About the Author

and understand the reasons why the relationship did not continue and flourish.

Marshaun understands what the average person looking for a meaningful, loving relationship normally goes through, especially when it comes to recognizing what they want, need, and desire. She understands what is holding men and women back from creating their healthy love life. She also knows how to steer them back onto their correct path. Marshaun combines all her data and research and shares simple tips and proven strategies with her clients, so they can stop being an obstacle in their own life and enjoy a great relationship.

Marshaun has a thriving YouTube channel and a list of growing clients. Her mission is to decrease the divorce rate and simultaneously increase the marriage rate. The best part of her job is seeing the change in her clients and their way of thinking after her coaching. She shares honest, straightforward, thought-provoking life experiences and advice both in her book and with her clients.

Marshaun resides in San Diego with her husband and their daughter.

Visit my website to set up a FREE Discovery Call for a step by step plan to create your love life ©
www.marshaunolaniyan.com

Get more awesome content on how to create a healthy romantic relationship at:
www.youtube.com/marshauno

www.ingramcontent.com/pod-product-compliance
Lightning Source LLC
LaVergne TN
LVHW041227080426
835508LV00011B/1104